PUT YOUR **MONEY** WHERE YOUR **HEART** IS

FINDING FINANCIAL HAPPINESS

SUE STEVENS

To Geri,

Thanks for your support as a mystic sister. My 2010 big new adventures, much joy and every financial happiness.

ISBN: 1-4392-6266-7
ISBN-13: 978-1-4392-6266-5
Library of Congress Control Number: 2009911612
Visit www.booksurge.com to order additional copies.

Designed by James Eaton Design
Typesetting by Jessica Sprong
Illustrations by Janice Fried

Grateful acknowledgment is made for permission to reprint
"NAPFA Comprehensive Financial Advisor Diagnostic."
Used by permission of Ellen Turf.

To Nancy Stevens, my mother,
who always puts her money where her heart is.

Table of Contents

vii   Introduction

1   Chapter One: The Other Gold
Looking Inside Your Heart

9   Chapter Two: The New American Dream
Living Within Your Means

19   Chapter Three: Where Is Your Money?
Creating and Interpreting Your Net Worth Statement

39   Chapter Four: Portfolio Peace of Mind™
A Fresh Approach to Money Management

77   Chapter Five: It's Not Just Retirement, It's the Rest of Your Life™
Take a Chance, Start Over, Reset your Compass

101   Chapter Six: The Financial Bridge™
Providing for Loved Ones After You're Gone

129   Chapter Seven: A Matter of Trust
Choosing a Financial Partner

137   Chapter Eight: Radiant Wealth™
Living A Life of Fulfillment

146   Appendix A: *The Independent Portfolio Assessment*

149   Appendix B: *NAPFA Comprehensive Financial Advisor Diagnostic*

156   Appendix C: *Recommended Reading*

157   Glossary

167   Acknowledgments

Introduction

Let's face it—much of the financial world is a mystery. It changes quickly, the terminology can be confusing, and it's easy to forget why you're doing this in the first place. *Put Your Money Where Your Heart Is™* focuses on what's truly important, gives you the tools to get organized, shows you how to interpret the results and shares inspirational stories of how people just like you have used these principles to change their lives for the better.

By thinking about what you want your money to do (for the people and causes you love the most), you can find deep satisfaction in how you lead your financial life. By choosing investments that speak to your heart and that may have socially conscious intentions, you can put your money to work in projects and technologies that can benefit not only your portfolio, but the world at large. When you know you have everything you truly need and you can extend that sense of fulfillment to enrich the lives of others, you will find financial happiness. You can choose to do that personally or charitably or perhaps both.

Stories bring these messages home. Let me share one with you now. You should know that all of the stories in this book are based on true situations I've experienced with clients. Unless the clients have requested I use their real names, I've changed them and any identifying information to protect confidentiality. Stories may be composites of several clients' experiences with the same goals and outcomes.

A well-known social activist came to me for investment advice a few years ago. I was shocked when I first looked at his portfolio. He had been a client of a large brokerage firm for years and they invested his money in separately managed accounts. (Basically that's a pool of investments that investors buy into.) In this case, the fees were too high, in my opinion, and many of the underlying investments were in direct conflict with this person's moral compass.

Now there's not necessarily anything "wrong" with separately managed accounts. But there is a problem with not knowing what your money is invested in and being uncomfortable knowing that your money is not consistent with how you live your life.

In repositioning this client's portfolio to better align with his values, we were able to sell AIG, Fannie Mae and GM before they imploded. We sold many mutual funds that had unnecessarily high fees. We sold stock in several defense contractors that were especially incongruent with his social consciousness. After all, how can you make a living talking about how the world needs to change and then invest your money in weapons of mass destruction?

We replaced those investments with a carefully constructed balanced portfolio with low expenses that incorporated socially conscious choices. We were able to do long-range planning that fused professional and personal objectives into one straight-forward vision that not only built the client's wealth, but allowed him to use his unique abilities to inspire and educate millions of other people.

The result is that this client now has Portfolio Peace of Mind™. He knows that his money reflects his overall attitude toward life and that allows him to focus on the love he brings to his work and the world at large.

There are lots of personal finance books available. They go into great detail about investment theory, estate planning techniques and all kinds of other advice. Those books are important and I'll share some of my favorites in the Recommended Reading portion of the Appendix.

But this book is going to cut right to what I consider to be the most important elements of bringing your financial life into congruence with what you believe. I'll present new paradigms and proprietary templates to challenge your thinking and help you organize your approach. I'll keep it relatively short and to the point. For additional resources, I'll point you in the right direction.

I have twenty years of experience in this field that allows me to distinguish what's really going to help you the most in the least amount of time. I've led teams of professionals in top financial organizations, managed millions of dollars that clients have entrusted me with, founded and written newsletters and columns that have been followed by hundreds of thousands of people. Now I want to share this information with you.

My Story

My path has been anything but traditional. I grew up in rather modest circumstances—and I'm grateful that I did. When you don't have a lot of money, you need to find other ways to entertain yourself. So I read library books. I learned how to play the cello. I helped my grandparents in our vegetable garden. I spent time outdoors in nature at the local parks and botanic gardens.

That was my family's legacy to me: to know how to enjoy the good things in life, without an emphasis on money. Education was highly valued in my family, so I learned to take advantage of books and classes to further myself in many valuable ways.

I started my professional career as a cellist. Yes, the big soulful instrument that was almost bigger than I was at ten years old. I've always had a bit of a rebellious nature, so when they threatened to kick me out of the middle school orchestra, I got mad and practiced. And practiced. And eventually did make my way to Carnegie Hall and many of the finest concert halls around the world playing with the New York String Orchestra, the Chicago Symphony Orchestra and many others. I completed my undergraduate degree in music at Northwestern University in Evanston, Illinois. I worked and played with the best—Sir Georg Solti, Leonard Bernstein, Seiji Ozawa, Carlo Maria Guilini, Daniel Barenboim, Luciano Pavarotti, Placido Domingo, Isaac Stern. Talk about an education.

It wasn't just classical music that I loved. I loved all kinds of music. I played on lots of pop, R&B—even country—albums and eventually became a member of The Recording Academy (you know—the folks that vote on the Grammy's). I had the honor of playing, touring and recording with Frank Sinatra, Tony Bennett, Mannheim Steamroller, Dionne Warwick, George Benson, Lyle Lovett, Smokey Robinson, Michael Bolton, Gladys Knight, Joel Grey, Richard Harris, David McCallum and many others. I made a brief appearance in Home Alone II and played on hundreds of TV and radio commercials made in the '80s. It was fun. It was rewarding. But eventually, it wasn't enough.

So I decided to make a quantum leap. I researched the types of fields that were predicted to be in demand over the next twenty years and found that financial advisors would be needed as the Baby Boomers started to retire. That sounded intriguing and I was fortunate to be accepted to one of the finest business schools in the country—especially in finance—and completed my MBA at The University of Chicago.

I'd always been pretty good at accumulating and investing my money, although I'd fallen victim to many of the same traps I suspect some of you have. Too much debt. Not enough savings. Not devoting enough time to staying on top of my finances.

But maybe that's in part what makes me qualified to write this book. I have made mistakes—and learned from them. What I've found is the wise use of money all boils down to knowing what you really want and not being afraid to take a well thought-out risk.

When I made my career change, for instance, I was worried that people might be skeptical about taking financial advice from a cellist, so I set about putting some credentials behind my name.

Even before I was hired by Arthur Andersen in their personal financial planning division, I began studying for the CPA exam. Good thing too. I passed on my first try—somewhat of a miracle as I look back on it now.

I also knew I wanted to be a CFP® professional, but at the time Arthur Andersen wouldn't pay for it. But that didn't stop me. I spent my own money (and time) studying for the exam. It took a couple years to complete the program, but I successfully passed all of the requirements.

I left Arthur Andersen in 1996 and took a job at The Vanguard Group. I moved to the Philadelphia area and worked on mass market financial planning products like websites, workbooks, educational newsletters, pamphlets and so forth. I had a great creative team and we took a great deal of satisfaction from the fact that we were doing work that helped people that really needed this type of guidance. We also won awards for the work we did.

While I was at Vanguard, I earned my Chartered Financial Analyst (CFA) designation. This credential focuses more on the investment side of "wealth management." I also had the great pleasure of watching one of my financial heroes, Jack Bogle, up close. Jack not only founded Vanguard, but revolutionized the mutual fund industry with his single-minded devotion to the individual investor.

But after three years of living in the beautiful rolling hills of Pennsylvania, I decided what I really loved was working one-on-one with individual clients. So it was time for another change.

I had always admired the folks at Morningstar. Don Phillips, Managing Director, Corporate Strategy, Research, and Communications and President of Fund Research, is very highly regarded, and is someone whose integrity I have always greatly admired. Joe Mansueto, Chairman and CEO, is the brother of one of my best friends (now deceased) and we all got to know each other over the years and shared a common bond through University of Chicago. The culture at Morningstar was more "liberal arts" than most corporations, so I found myself more at home there.

We worked out a somewhat non-traditional arrangement. When I started at Morningstar in 1999, I worked four days a week for them and was able to start up my own private financial advisory practice. The lawyers blessed the arrangement and sealed it with a contract. Over the years, many of Morningstar's talented, creative people have become not only good friends but clients. I left Morningstar at the end of 2007, but continue to contribute to www.morningstar.com as a guest author.

For the past twenty years, I've been privileged to work with hundreds of individual investors directly, listen to thousands of you as Director of Financial Planning at Morningstar and develop mass market resources during my years at The Vanguard Group. All of these roles have provided me with the opportunity to help people find what's important to them and support that through sound financial decision-making.

So that brings you up to today. I wrote a successful, award-winning column for www.morningstar.com for nine years. I launched, authored and edited Morningstar's personal finance newsletter *Practical Finance*. My private practice, Stevens Wealth Management, has grown to where I manage over $150 million on a daily basis with the help of a very talented staff. My personal finance e-newsletter, *Radiant Wealth*™, goes out to over 100,000 readers every month. And I've created a financial education website, www.financial-happiness.com, that offers continued opportunity for growth and learning about personal finance.

I've earned my MBA, CERTIFIED FINANCIAL PLANNER™ mark, CPA/PFS, CFA and an MS in Wealth Management. I've been named one of the top advisors in the country multiple times by *Worth, Forbes, Bloomberg, Reuters* and others. In 2008 I was named one of the Top 50 Distinguished Women in Wealth Management by *Wealth Manager Magazine*. I've been quoted in *The Wall Street Journal, New York Times, Chicago Tribune, Baltimore Sun, Boston Globe, Washington Post, Journal for Financial Planning, AARP, Business Week, Forbes* and many others.

So I know my financial stuff, but my story goes far beyond number crunching. I care about creating an atmosphere that inspires and encourages personal development and enrichment. And toward that end, I've attended teachings by His Holiness The Dalai Lama, studied mysticism and soul development with Caroline Myss and Andrew Harvey, taken doctorate level classes on the ancient levels of the humanities in Chartres outside of Paris and participated in the launch of the Institute for Sacred Activism. I am fortunate to have a close group of soul companions that meet in the Chicago suburbs on a monthly basis. We support each other through life's challenges and cheer each other on through our successes and accomplishments.

For me, the sacred also includes my animal family. So often we neglect to consider the needs of these soul teachers and companions, so the section of this book on Animal Grace offers ideas on how to care for them even after we're gone.

I'm also grateful for a loving family and a vibrant musical life. The two have been combined for me and have offered great lessons and opportunities for growth. And finally I am very grateful for my staff at Stevens Wealth

Management and Financial Happiness®. Without all of these people and influences, none of this would be possible.

People are the most rewarding part of this business for me. I have twenty years of experience to share with you, but more importantly I want to encourage you to find new ways to think about traditional topics. I've learned money means different things to different people and that you can't define success for you by anyone else's standards.

To live content with small means,
To seek elegance rather than luxury,
And refinement rather than fashion,
To be worthy, not respectable, and wealthy, not rich,
To study hard, think quietly, talk gently, act frankly,
To listen to stars and birds, babes and sages, with open heart,
To bear all cheerfully,
Do all bravely,
Await occasions,
Hurry never—
In a word, to let the spiritual, unbidden and unconscious,
Grow up through the common.
This is to be my symphony.
~William Ellery Channing, *Earth Prayers*

Your Story

Enough about me. This book is about you. You can have everything that's really important to you. But you need to do some soul searching, commit at least a little time to sorting out your personal finances and make some changes to how you align your values and your money.

This book is for people:

- » Looking for something more personally satisfying and rewarding in their lives
- » Ready to embrace a new approach to structuring their financial concerns
- » Who are serious about finding financial happiness
- » Who believe money can and should be used to support your highest intentions

This book will:

- » Inspire you to reflect on what matters to you
- » Challenge you to make changes to align your use of money with your values
- » Show you a new approach to budgeting
- » Teach you how to examine your Net Worth for balance
- » Introduce you to a six-step process to achieve Portfolio Peace of Mind™
- » Share stories of how people changed the course of their destinies
- » Give you tools and resources to help your loved ones after you die
- » Help you find financial happiness and reach a state of "Radiant Wealth™"

Why this approach now?

Many people find personal finance dry and lifeless. It doesn't have to be that way. It's really about your life and how to make it more rewarding and enjoyable. By paying attention to a few key areas, you can transform your everyday relationship with money from frustrating to inspiring. Instead of endless worry, you can create a life that you look forward to living because it reflects who you are and what is important to you.

If you want to make a difference in the world, then you need to start with yourself. You must take responsibility for your own financial choices. This can make a profound impact on the world. How you invest your money is every bit as important, and perhaps more important, as how you cast your vote.

It's just that simple.

A Surprise of Roses

A long cry at midnight near the mosque, a dying cry.
The young man sitting there

Hears and thinks, "That sound doesn't make me afraid.
Why should it?

It's the drumbeat announcing a celebration! It means
We should start cooking

The joy soup!" He hears beyond his death fear to the
Union. "It's time

For that merging in me now." He jumps up and shouts to
God, "If you can be human, come

Inside me now!" The signal of the death yell splits him
Open. The mystery pours from all

Directions, gold coins, liquid gold, gold cloth, gold bars.
They pile up blocking

The doors to the mosque. The young man works all night
Carrying the gold away in sacks,

Burying it, and coming back for more. The timid congregation
Sleeps through it all.

If you think I'm talking about actual gold, you're like those
Children who pretend

That pieces of broken dishes are money, so that anytime they
See pottery shards they think

Of money, as when you hear the word gold and wish for it. This
Is the other gold,

That glows in your chest when you love. The enchanted mosque
Is in there too, where

The pointed cry is a candle flame on the altar. The young man
Becomes a moth who gambles himself

And wins. A true human being is not human! This candle does
Not burn. It illuminates.

Some candles burn themselves and one another up. Others
Taste like a surprise of

Roses in a room, and you just a stranger who wandered in.

~ Jelaluddin Rumi

Chapter 1

The Other Gold

Looking Inside Your Heart

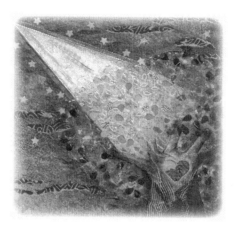

C reating wealth is all about finding "the other gold." The gold that comes from within. Because as an investment advisor for the past twenty years, I can tell you no matter how much money you have, it's what's in your heart that matters. That's why I'm taking the time to devote a chapter to thinking about how to approach your financial decisions. Then we'll move on to number crunching.

We've seen tremendous change take place in the financial world and in the world at large, and it's only going to accelerate. What we've counted on in the past will look different going forward. That can be disconcerting and at times alarming.

All the more reason to put your money where your heart is. What I mean by that is that despite all the chaos in the world around you, focus on what you love. Your family. Animals. The environment. The arts. Charities. Your work. Whatever is meaningful to you.

Your investments need to support that love. It's not just a matter of accumulating as much as possible. That misses the point entirely. Think about what you need your money to do: provide an income stream; give you a base that allows you to try something new; give your loved ones a chance in life they wouldn't have otherwise; find the joy that comes from giving to others.

Resetting Our Internal Compass

Success is not the key to happiness. Happiness is the key to success.
~ Albert Schweitzer

The recent stock market shock waves are a wake-up call to re-set our priorities. Yes, we have recovery ahead of us. And we'll need to save more than ever to make up part of what we've lost. But we also have the opportunity to re-examine how we want to do this.

My friend Kay, a marketing guru, suggested that I write something summarizing how you find financial happiness. What I realized is that whether it's "financial happiness®" or just plain old "happiness," the steps are really the same.

Timeless truths work across mediums. I've seen how harmony works in the music business, in the world of mysticism and in balancing portfolios. Try applying these jewels to your daily routines and see how life gets even better.

Ten Paths to Financial Happiness®

1. Start the day with gratitude.
Intention is everything. His Holiness The Dalai Lama starts his day with meditation that can last several hours. You probably can't do that, but start with a simple "thank you" as you think about everything that you are grateful for.

As we've all had to adjust to the stock market crash, it's made me re-think how I define "success." Success is being congruent with what you intend to do. In my business life, it makes me grateful for my clients, my conservative approach and my loyal, hard-working staff.

I also know I have everything I need. We live in a country of magnificent abundance. The economic derailment helped put some things in perspective. Being grateful for a job, health insurance, family and friends to lend a hand as needed. And if we don't have some of those things right now, at least we have the possibility of obtaining them some day.

One thing I've learned over the years is that whenever I'm in a particularly blue mood, nothing helps more than thinking about ten things I'm grateful for—except maybe a nap. You can count the ten financial (or even non-financial) things you value most to help boost your gratitude level.

2. Surrender to what you can't control.

Grant me the serenity to accept the things I cannot change,
the courage to change the things I can,
and the wisdom to know the difference.
~ The Serenity Prayer

You need to get real about what you can control and what you can't. Many of us are control freaks, so this isn't easy.

You can't control the stock market. Or the weather. Or the economy.

You can control your reaction to just about anything. You can control costs. You can plan for at least some contingencies.

The key is focusing on what you need to be happy, making that as foolproof as possible and stop worrying about everything that can go wrong.

3. Increase your confidence through learning more.

In Malcolm Gladwell's *Outliers, The Story of Success,* Chapter Two is devoted to "The 10,000-Hour Rule." Psychologist K. Anders Ericsson conducted a study of musicians to examine the roles of innate talent and the role of preparation.

What they found is that it takes about 10,000 hours of preparation to be good at just about anything. That goes for music, basketball, writing, you name it. Having had several very different careers, that seems about right to me. It takes diligence and practice.

So why would finance be any different? If you want to feel confident about your money, you've got to spend time on it. In most cases, you should try to devote at least an hour a week to paying attention to what needs to be done.

That's not just on your portfolio, but on all of your personal finance needs.

It helps to read about financial topics too. *The Wall Street Journal* is a good start. A subscription to *Radiant Wealth*™ (www.financial-happiness.com) wouldn't hurt either. The more you are familiar with the terminology and types of common occurrences, the less panicked you'll feel as you watch the media rant and rave about what happened that week. Maybe you'll eventually feel you can just turn that noise off. Because most of the time, that's all it is.

Of course you need to know what's going on. But you need discernment to help distinguish what's really important from what's just a blip on the radar this week.

4. Focus on healthy balance.

This is one of my mantras. Balance seems to be a true secret of happiness. Too much work or too much food or too much of anything just isn't sustainable. You can't make sound decisions unless you balance the physical, mental, emotional and spiritual needs in your life. So make time for all of these activities.

You also need to balance your assets and your liabilities. Whoever let people borrow beyond their means in the real estate melt-down didn't understand balance. Even if someone agrees to lend you more money, don't take it unless you can truly manage the debt load. And not just paying the interest only.

Balance is key in finding Portfolio Peace of Mind™. You need to know that you have a good mix of stocks, bonds and cash that allows you to sleep at night. It's a balancing act between risk and reward.

Even budgeting requires balance. In *The New American Dream* (Chapter Two), I talk about how every household needs to spread their money across all of Maslow's hierarchy of needs. How much you spend per category will vary depending on how much you have to work with, but all those needs should be covered.

5. Don't rule anything out. Miracles are possible.

Once you set your intention, try assuming that somehow, someway, you can accomplish what your mind may tell you can't be done. Strangely enough, things may happen during the day that you couldn't have anticipated and amazing things can be achieved. It's a little bit like bending time and space.

Dare to dream. Take a chance. Yes, you'll fail sometimes. But the joy of succeeding—especially against the odds—makes it all the sweeter.

Just make sure that you stack the deck in your favor by working hard, planning, anticipating problems and going the extra mile when things get tough. Don't just take wild gambles that aren't carefully researched and evaluated.

6. Let go of what you no longer need.

Doesn't it feel good to clean out a closet or a drawer? Releasing what you no longer need is key to making room for what is new. It's true for relationships, gardens, garages and portfolios.

The Chinese would call this good feng shui. In the world of finance, it means clearing out what you no longer need. Here's what you can throw out:

» Marketing materials and envelope stuffers.
» Most cancelled checks. But keep any cancelled checks you need to support tax deductions, insurance claims or the cost basis of your home.
» ATM receipts. Once you've reconciled your bank statements, shred these.
» Annual reports. Read these when you get them and then recycle them.
» Proxies. Either cast your vote right away or toss them.
» Old paid bills. You might want to keep the past year's bills and anything to support your prior year tax deductions.
» Old pay stubs. Keep one year's worth to reconcile with your employer's W-2 form.
» Credit card receipts. Match your receipts to your monthly statements when you get them. If they match up, you can shred the receipts unless you need them to document something like your tax-related expenses, insurance claims or the cost basis of your home. Save receipts for major purchases until the warranties expire.

When you rebalance your portfolio, you have another chance to release what you no longer need. I try to do this in the fall when I consider tax loss harvesting. If you are carrying large capital loss carry forwards on your tax return, you may want to think about "gain harvesting." But don't just do it for tax reasons. Make sure it makes sense for the portfolio too.

You may also need to let go of old attitudes about money. Maybe you didn't have enough growing up. Or maybe you blame someone (or even yourself) for set-backs you've encountered. Get over it. Move on. Let it go. Practice the Buddhist way of detachment. It works wonders for happiness.

7. Do what you love.

If you do what you love, you'll walk into your destiny—what you were born to do with your life. This can happen at any age, so don't think it's too late. Invoking your destiny begins with intention. You need to think about exactly what it is that interests and excites you. It may mean that you need to change your life and it can demand self-sacrifice. If you're thinking about making a big change, consider consulting with a financial advisor who can help you weigh the trade-offs before you take the plunge.

8. Forgive.

> *Without forgiveness there is no future.*
> ~ Archbishop Desmond Tutu

If you genuinely want happiness (financial or otherwise), you need to learn to forgive. Whatever the injustice, harboring it only gives it more power. Let it go.

Use your precious energy to build up your strengths. What are you good at? How can you increase your gifts? Don't let old feelings drag you down.

Forgiveness comes from within. And it's a two-way street. You need to forgive yourself too. Sometimes you're your own worst critic.

Once you've forgiven, you can move on with your life. And sometimes it helps other people move on with their lives too. You'll have more energy to give to what matters in your life right now.

Forgiveness is first for you, the forgiver, to release you
from something that will eat you alive; that will destroy
your joy and your ability to love fully and openly.
~ Wm. Paul Young, *The Shack*

9. Connect and find inspiration.

Connect with anything or anybody that feeds your soul. Perhaps you enjoy spending quiet time in nature. Or being with people or a community that can support one another on life's journey. Maybe you have discovered meditation or prayer that helps center you. Some people find inspiration through exercise.

Most of us need connection with something greater than ourselves. Inspiration gives you the courage to try again. That can help after the stock market knocks the wind out of you or something else in life sets you back. Once you can get past the fear and frustration, your heart knows what to do next. It never fails.

Listen to your heart. It knows all things, because it came
from the Soul of the World, and it will one day return there.
~ Paul Coelho, *The Alchemist*

10. Put your money where your heart is.

Aligning your financial matters with your values and hopes for your life make it so much more congruent, meaningful and joyful. You reflect the love that is given to you in your actions that can support so much more than you.

If you can follow even a few of these paths, your life will increase in happiness. Extend them to how you conduct your financial life and you will find financial happiness. But even that is not enough. Once you find happiness, you must enjoy it. We've forgotten this essential teaching in our quest to acquire more and more.

For if Happiness be worthy to be sought, it is worthy to be enjoyed.
As no folly in the world is more vile than that pretended by alche-
mists, of having the Philosopher's Stone and being contented without
using it: so is no deceit more odious, than that of spending many
days in studying, and none in enjoying, happiness.
~ Thomas Traherne, *Centuries of Meditation*

The Other Gold

To be congruent in your life, you need to be clear about what you love and your actions need to support your intentions. Your money, in a sense, represents how you choose to direct your energy. It starts with a vision of where you want to go. As you spend time reflecting on what's most important to you, what's happening in the world around you and how you plan to take action going forward, an inner metamorphosis is unveiled.

So *Put Your Money Where Your Heart Is* is about expressing your love for life through your money. That may seem like a foreign concept, but how better to make yourself heard than through one of the most powerful mediums we have at our disposal? **Something as simple as a person's investment can be just as powerful as their vote.** One of our summer interns, Andrew Welter, wrote these words as part of his summer writing assignment. It's pure genius.

> *It is in surrender to this greatest of all Laws of Alchemy that we discover and become the real gold, discover and become the real power, the real hope. The terrible crisis we have manifested out of the addictions of our false self, if we learn its lessons, will lead us out of darkness into Light, out of the darkness of a relentless egoism that fuels destruction into a Light in which all we are and do can turn increasingly to divine gold and "en-golden" life on earth.*
> ~ Andrew Harvey, *The Hope*

Throughout the book I'll be recommending other books that I think are valuable contributions to our profession and worth your time to read. Two that relate to this first chapter are George Kinder's *Lighting the Torch* and Brent Kessel's *It's Not About the Money*. George and Brent understand "The Other Gold" and have dedicated their professions to promoting awareness about why we seek to grow our wealth. Both books are referenced in Appendix C.

Now let's turn our attention in Chapter Two to something very basic—budgeting. But with a twist. Whether you've stuck to a budget your whole life or you've never thought about it at all, this fresh approach will challenge you to examine how you choose to direct your cash flow. That's the first step toward balance and putting your money where your heart is.

The New American Dream

Living Within Your Means

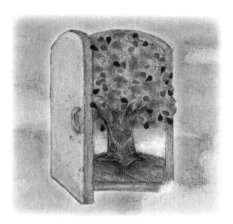

O ne of my clients lived in a small farm house for 40 years of his life. They were the best years of his life. Like many people, he longed for the day when he could build the house of his dreams. It would have everything he ever wanted—a great view, huge floor-to-ceiling windows, the best that money could buy.

And he did it. The house is built. The view is spectacular. But in spite of all the careful planning, my client isn't happy. He looks around every day and thinks this house is not a true reflection of who he is and his values.

That classic American Dream is not his American Dream. My job is to help him reassess how that house fits into his overall financial picture. We need to think about building a New American Dream.

The recent credit crisis has shown that owning a big car and a house in the suburbs is not for everyone. In fact, it has created a financial nightmare for millions of Americans.

In other words, it has pulled us away from our hearts. The New American Dream is one where we learn to manage our money responsibly. We allocate our money to what we value the most. We live within our means. We don't live on more credit than we can comfortably manage. We make whatever adjustments are necessary to get back on track.

> *Our ultimate aim in seeking more wealth*
> *is a sense of satisfaction, of happiness.*
> *But the very basis of seeking more*
> *is a feeling of not having enough,*
> *a feeling of discontentment.*
> *That feeling of discontentment,*
> *of wanting more and more and more,*
> *doesn't arise from the inherent desirability*
> *of the objects we are seeking,*
> *but rather from our own mental state.*
> ~ His Holiness The Dalai Lama, *The Art of Happiness*

The Purpose of Money

Money is the currency of American life. It drives how we spend our time and it has the power to bring us joy or frustration. For too long, far too many of us have bought into the myth that buying more things will satisfy an emotional need or build our self worth. Perhaps it's time to find a new way to look at the purpose of money in our lives.

To do that, a certain amount of introspection is called for. And it makes sense to base our choices on what we truly need. It occurred to me that it might help to merge the exercise of budgeting with the psychology of what human beings need. That led me to Maslow's hierarchy of needs, which you may remember from your college psychology class.

Abraham Maslow wrote a paper in 1943 entitled *A Theory of Human Motivation* that described a five-stage model that builds level-upon-level in this sequence of needs: physiological, security, love/belonging, esteem and self-actualization.

We can use the Maslow model to help us reconsider how we choose to spend our money. Of course we need to make sure our basic physiological and security needs are met. But all of us also need to allocate some of our hard-earned cash to the higher levels of the hierarchy too.

The Financial Hierarchy of Needs

What we're really talking about here is budgeting. And you can take a look at any number of credit counseling services or financial guidelines that give you guidance about how much money is prudent to spend on various financial needs. But none of them address how those categories relate to our human needs.

The following model fuses our needs as human beings with a common sense approach to how we allocate our money:

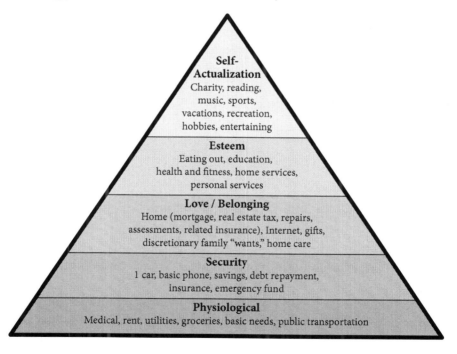

Self-Actualization
Charity, reading, music, sports, vacations, recreation, hobbies, entertaining

Esteem
Eating out, education, health and fitness, home services, personal services

Love / Belonging
Home (mortgage, real estate tax, repairs, assessments, related insurance), Internet, gifts, discretionary family "wants," home care

Security
1 car, basic phone, savings, debt repayment, insurance, emergency fund

Physiological
Medical, rent, utilities, groceries, basic needs, public transportation

Let's take a look at how you might categorize typical expenses across Maslow's five levels of basic human needs:

Physiological

The most basic needs are food, water, sleep, shelter, health care and so forth. Perhaps you don't need to own a home at this level, but you need a roof over your head. If you have children, you obviously need to provide basic care. You need to be able to get around, but not everyone will need to own a car. Public transportation offers a viable alternative for some.

Security

Next on the ladder of needs is security. This starts with building up an emergency fund to cover at least three months (and hopefully a year) of expenses. That provides security should you encounter an unexpected large expense or if you lose your job. Security also includes a regular savings program where you bank at least 10% of your net income (gross income less income tax). If you've amassed debt, this is where you build in debt repayment monthly (although you may choose to put your mortgage payment in the next category). Many people will also want to include basic types of insurance to provide security for themselves and their families as well as owning a car and having basic phone service.

Love/Belonging

Love can mean many things. Providing care and comfort for those you love. Creating memories that may not even cost a dime. It can also mean creating a sense of community and, in some cases, buying a home. If you choose to buy versus rent, you'll need to allocate money for mortgage payments, real estate taxes, repairs, assessments and related insurance. Love/Belonging may also include Internet charges (your electronic community), gifts, discretionary family "wants" and support services.

Esteem

It's amazing how much money we spend trying to make ourselves feel better. Self-esteem activities are in the eye of the beholder, but may include eating out, higher education (this could fit in multiple categories), health and fitness, home services and personal care services.

Self-Actualization

This final level is where we express ourselves as individuals. That may be through giving our time and money to others through charity or in self-development that stretches our potential. These activities can be anything that elevates the human spirit like reading, movies, music, sporting events, vacations, recreation, hobbies or entertaining.

Hierarchy of Needs Budgeting

As you might imagine, when you have less money, more of it will probably go toward the first levels of the hierarchy. With more money, the proportion spent on basic needs can be less. But people of all levels of wealth have the same needs and should make sure they allocate some money to each area.

The following is a guideline for how you might allocate your money to the different levels in the hierarchy depending on how much you have to work with. Remember that you start with your net income: your total income less income taxes. Apply that figure to the percentages in the table *(see table on p.14).*

This is meant as a starting place as you think about your own life and how you might allocate your money. You spend only what you take home. You create a vision of how to balance what you have to work with so that you meet every level of human need. You learn to live within your means and find satisfaction with what you have.

Enjoying Your Money

While I'm all for responsibly allocating your money across your needs, it doesn't mean that there isn't room for a little fun now and then. Sometimes money should just be enjoyed. We get so serious about it much of the time. There are times when hard work deserves a special reward.

Budgeting by Hierarchy of Needs

	Entry Level $30,000 to $50,000 net		Comfort Level $60,000 to $90,000 net		Luxury Level $100,000 to $150,000+ net	
Physiological						
Rent	20%					
Utilities – heat, water, gas, electric, etc	4%		5%		5%	
Groceries	8%		8%		5%	
Basic Needs (kids, pets, clothing, etc.)	7%	55%	8%	30%	8%	25%
Public Transportation	5%					
Medical	5%		5%		5%	
Other	6%		4%		2%	
Security						
Phone	2%		2%		2%	
Car – insurance, gas, etc. (1 car per person)			7%		7%	
Debt Payments	5%	15%	5%	25%	5%	25%
Savings (goal of 10% net income)	5%		10%		10%	
Other	3%		1%		1%	
Love / Belonging						
Mortgage, Real Estate Tax, Repairs, Assessments, Insurance			20%		20%	
Internet	At Your Discretion	10%	1%	25%	1%	30%
Gifts			3%		3%	
Other (extras for kids)			1%		6%	
Esteem						
Eating Out			5%		3%	
Education	At Your Discretion	10%	2%	10%	3%	10%
Health & Fitness			2%		3%	
Other			1%		1%	
Self Actualization						
Charity						
Music, Books						
Cable, Satellite	At Your Discretion	10%	At Your Discretion	10%	At Your Discretion	10%
Concerts, Sports						
Vacations						
Other (additional phones, cars, gifts, etc.)						

Approximate percentages per category

The Little Red Boxster

"Consider a workaholic married to a self-employed tool dealer. We know how to work hard and have been fortunate to have that produce the opportunity for financial security – if we tend to our investments prudently. Neither of us had the background to do that without significant learning and time commitment – which we didn't have. We turned to Stevens Wealth Management.

As Sue got to know our financial objectives, she also got to know us as people. So, when a neighbor decided to move back to France and needed to sell that sporty little Boxster convertible quickly we turned to Sue to help break the deadlock on the home front (to buy or not to buy). Her wise counsel: 'Finances are there to enjoy and you can afford to do things like this occasionally. You're not the type to make a habit of it (nor should you!) so, in this case, live a little and enjoy it. I can't wait to see the car!'

Based on her advice, we did buy the car, we are enjoying a prudent lifestyle that includes doing the things we are passionate about (with the top down and in a down market), and are confident that she will provide wise counsel when we need it – even if we don't ask for it!"

Your Challenge

The best way to learn about personal finance is to apply it to your own situation. You need to know where your money is going. Get your checkbook and your credit card statements for at least the past three months (one year is even better). Group your expenses by the hierarchy of needs. You can find an electronic template to use at www.financial-happiness.com. We've also included a print copy for you on the following page.

Budgeting by Hierarchy of Needs Worksheet

Estimated Monthly Net $: _____	Estimated Monthly Expenses $	%	Target %	Difference (in $)
Physiological				
Rent				
Utilities – heat, water, gas, electric, etc				
Groceries				
Basic Needs (kids, pets, clothing, etc.)				
Public Transportation				
Medical				
Other				
Subtotal :				
Security				
Phone				
Car – insurance, gas, etc. (1 car per person)				
Debt Payments				
Savings (goal of 10% net income)				
Other				
Subtotal :				
Love / Belonging				
Mortgage, Real Estate Tax, Repairs, Assessments, Insurance				
Internet				
Gifts				
Other (extras for kids)				
Subtotal :				
Esteem				
Eating Out				
Education				
Health & Fitness				
Other				
Subtotal :				
Self Actualization				
Charity				
Music, Books				
Cable, Satellite				
Concerts, Sports				
Vacations				
Other (additional phones, cars, gifts, etc.)				
Subtotal :				
Grand Total :				

Instructions for Budgeting By Hierarchy of Needs Worksheet

Step 1:   Enter your estimated monthly net income. That's what you bring home after-tax.

Step 2:   Enter your monthly expenses by category. (The electronic worksheet at www.financial-happiness.com will do the math for you.)

Step 3:   Enter your target percentages by category. This is your intention for each category.

Step 4:   Make any changes to how you want to allocate your money in the far right column.

Interpreting the Results

Once you've completed the exercise, ask yourself some questions. Are you surprised about where your money is going? Are you conscious about it? Are you happy with the allocation of your money across your hierarchy of needs? Do you want to make some changes? What are the top three things you can do right away to feel better about how you are spending your money?

The point of this exercise is to reflect on what is important and meaningful to you and then to analyze how your money is spent. From there you can make choices about how you shape your American Dream.

The New American Dream is to build a solid financial base by choosing how we allocate our money and living on what we take home from our jobs or withdraw in retirement. What the credit crisis has hopefully taught us is that buying a house you really can't afford or accumulating debt you can't easily repay isn't a healthy way to live. We can meet our hierarchy of needs in a more meaningful and affordable way.

Make sure you are saving—that's the key to future success. If you can't save 10% of net income right away, start with a level you can commit to and increase it by 1% or more every chance you get.

Just about everyone is paying attention to what they spend now. Tougher times and reduced asset balances will do that. Find ways to inspire yourself as you get more responsible about how you choose to use your money. You can't control what happens in the stock market or what you pay in tax, but you can control what you spend. And still have everything you need!

Using this type of model lets you allocate your money thoughtfully to both what you need and what you love. As you grow in controlling how you use your own money, you'll also move closer to being in a position to help others with their financial lives too.

Reflecting on how you budget your cash flow is just your first step. Next, in Chapter Three, you will turn your attention to what you own and what you owe. This snapshot in time gives you a good picture of where you stand financially. With some help on interpreting this information, you can see how to shape these building blocks of your life.

Chapter 3

Where is Your Money?

Creating and Interpreting Your Net Worth Statement

W hat is your net worth telling you? Living in a culture that's pre-occupied with consumption, it sometimes seems we're judged on how big our balance sheet is rather than how big our hearts are. It's far too easy to get down on ourselves because we think we don't measure up, as defined by what we see in television commercials, which of course isn't reality at all. It doesn't have to be that way

What I've discovered is that the number of zeros you have behind your net worth has virtually no bearing on how much good you can do in the world. And your net worth isn't a reflection of your self-worth.

But the fact remains that if you want to be financially independent, you'll need to build up your assets—put down your financial roots. It also helps to recognize any red flags in your financial picture that could derail your future.

That's what the Net Worth Statement can do for you. Think of your net worth as a snapshot in time that captures everything you own less what you owe. Your Net Worth Statement helps you see where you stand and from there you can figure out where you want to go. It also allows you to perceive patterns that may not be healthy or sustainable. By recognizing this early, you can make changes to how you are managing your money.

Know What You Own and What You Owe

To complete the Net Worth Statement, gather this information:

✓ Any brokerage or investment statements

✓ Savings, CD and money market balances

✓ Life insurance declaration pages

✓ Retirement plan statements

✓ Mortgage and home equity statements and/or loan documents

✓ Credit card balances

✓ Home and personal property values

Your next step will be to fill in the Net Worth Statement (NWS) with this information. If you'd rather do this electronically, use our template at www.financial-happiness.com. For space reasons, the NWS in the book combines assets into one total per couple. The electronic NWS allows you to list assets by individual ownership. This allows you to see how much is in each spouse's name which is important to understand for estate planning purposes.

I'll walk you through each section of the NWS and then we'll talk about how to interpret the numbers. Check the glossary at the end of this book if you see an unfamiliar term.

As you complete the Net Worth Statement, only include assets in your ownership or your spouse's ownership. Do not include assets that belong to your children or your parents.

(See pages 22 and 23 for the Net Worth Statement)

Eight Steps to Completing
Your Net Worth Statement

1. Cash

When you begin thinking about your money, a good place to start is your liquidity. Our culture has it backwards: It seemingly rewards illiquidity by giving us too much access to credit. "Put no money down," is a constant refrain. But if you stop to think about it, such a strategy is not going to help you better control your financial life or offer financial freedom.

Liquid cash assets are types of accounts that you can get your hands on quickly and that are typically "safe" from the vagaries of the markets. Assets like money markets, checking accounts, savings accounts, credit union accounts, short-term Certificates of Deposit (CDs that mature in one year or less) fall into this category. These are the "positive" balances that make up your liquid cash assets.

The "negative" balances are things like credit card debt and money you owe other people (but not for homes or autos—that's covered later). If you have more in this type of debt than you do in liquid cash assets, then you have "negative liquidity." When you're young (and I'm typically thinking about people in their 20s), it's not unusual to have negative liquidity in your cash accounts. All that means is that you owe more than you hold in cash assets. But if you're older and in this situation, it's to your advantage to get out from under that much debt as quickly as possible.

2. Fixed Income and Equities

Bonds (fixed income) and stocks (equities) are "marketable" assets. They can be converted to cash, but it may take a little time.

So when we talk about building emergency reserves, you'll want to keep those in cash accounts like money markets. As you build your overall taxable accounts, you'll add to your "marketable" assets by holding more stocks and bonds—often in the form of mutual funds or exchange-traded funds.

When you list your stocks and bonds in the Net Worth Statement (and whenever I say "stocks and bonds," I mean mutual funds too), I suggest you

Your Name: Net Worth Statement as of:		Total by Category	% of Assets
Taxable Accounts		$	%
Cash		$	
CDs that Mature in Under One Year	$		
Checking	$		
Credit Union	$		
Money Markets	$		
Receivables You Expect to Collect	$		
Less: Major Credit Card Debt	$		
Less: Other Debt, Not Real Estate/Auto	$		
Fixed Income		$	
CDs that Mature in Over One Year	$		
Bond Mutual Funds by Brokerage Account	$		
Individual Bonds by Brokerage Account	$		
Savings Bonds	$		
Equities		$	
Individual Stocks by Brokerage Account	$		
Stock Mutual Funds by Brokerage Account	$		
Retirement Accounts		$	%
Traditional IRAs	$		
Roth IRAs	$		
401(k)s, 403(b)s, 457s	$		
Less: Outstanding Loans	$		
Pension Plans	$		
Annuities	$		
~ Fixed	$		
~ Variable	$		
Company Accounts		$	%
Company Stock	$		
Stock Options	$		
Incentive Options	$		
Vested	$		
Non-Vested	$		
Non-Qualified Options	$		
Vested	$		
Non-Vested	$		
Restricted Stock	$		
Capital Contributions	$		
Other Ownership Interests	$		
Less: Liabilities or Debt Personally Owed	$		

	Total by Category	% of Assets
Real Estate	$	%
Personal Residence	$	
Less: Mortgage	$	
Less: Home Equity Line of Credit	$	
Second Home	$	
Less: Mortgage	$	
Investment Properties	$	
REITs (not held in mutual funds)	$	
Real Estate Limited Partnerships	$	
Personal Property	$	%
Art	$	
Antiques	$	
Automobiles	$	
Less: Loan	$	
Boats	$	
Less: Loan	$	
Furniture and Household Goods	$	
Jewelry	$	
Musical Instruments	$	
Less: Loan	$	
Other Collectibles	$	
NET WORTH	$	$	%
Life Insurance Death Benefit	$	%
Term Life	$	
Whole Life	$	
Less: Outstanding Loans	$	
Other Types Of Life Insurance	$	
Less: Outstanding Loans	$	
ESTIMATED TOTAL ESTATE	$	

Electronic versions of this worksheet are available at www.financial-happiness.com
As you complete the Net Worth Statement, only include assets in your ownership or your spouse's ownership. Do not include assets that belong to your children or your parents.

categorize them by where they are held. For example, if I own three stock mutual funds at Vanguard, I would list:

Vanguard Mutual Funds	$ 35,000

Or if you want to be more detailed, you could list each holding separately.

Vanguard	
Vanguard Total Stock Market	$ 15,000
Vanguard Total International Stock Market	10,000
Vanguard Precious Metals & Mining	10,000

You may want to separate your fixed income holdings by how they are taxed. For example, if you own municipal ("muni") bonds you may want to total up their value and list them like this:

Schwab Muni Bonds	$ 100,000

Once you've entered cash accounts, fixed income and equities, you can total up what you own (net of related debt) in Taxable Accounts on the Net Worth Statement.

3. Retirement Accounts

The next couple types of assets are considered "restricted." Typically you can't have access to retirement accounts until you are at least age 55 (and more likely age 59 ½). These assets are treated differently from a tax perspective too. Most of these accounts will be taxed when you take the money out. For our purposes in the Net Worth Statement, enter the full pre-tax balance. Just keep in mind, Uncle Sam will come calling one day for his due.

Many of you will have IRAs (individual retirement accounts). Let's separate those into traditional IRAs and Roth IRAs (because they are taxed differently). If you have rollover IRAs, those would be considered "traditional." If you have an inherited IRA, list that separately unless you received it from your spouse. As a surviving spouse, you can roll over your spouse's IRA into your own IRA (this is true for a traditional or Roth IRA). If you have multiple IRA accounts, you can combine them by type (traditional or

Roth) and list them by ownership.

If you have an employer-sponsored retirement account like a 401(k), 403(b) or 457 plan, enter your current balance. You'll also want to indicate if you have a loan out against your plan (if you do, then include the full amount of the account as if the loan were paid back on the first line and the outstanding loan as a subtraction on the second line). You should see the overall retirement plan balance increase from year-to-year as you contribute to your plan (of course, the balance can go down depending on your investment experience).

Some of you will have pension plans. These are typically "defined benefit" plans and most companies don't offer them anymore. If you are allowed to take a "lump sum" from your pension plan, list that balance in your Net Worth Statement. Many of you in this situation will probably roll over your lump sum to an IRA. (The alternative distribution option is to receive a fixed amount over a period of years in retirement.) After you roll over your pension plan, you will owe tax as you take distributions. If you take the lump sum all at once (and don't roll it over), you'll owe tax on the full amount immediately.

4. Employer Stock and Stock Options

Not all of you will have this type of asset. If you don't, just skip to the next section. If you do have company assets, you should list them here. If you own employer stock outright, list it as a separate line item.

If you own employer stock in a retirement plan, just list the full value of the plan under Retirement Assets. If you have a choice, try not to hold more than 10% of your plan in employer stock. Keep this 10% guideline in mind for your overall portfolio too.

If you have stock options, you'll need to do a little math to capture their true value. First, identify if you have incentive stock options or non-qualified options. They are taxed differently, so you want to list each on its own line. In either case however, you need to know three things: the current price of the stock, the exercise price and the number of shares that are vested and non-vested. To calculate the value, use this formula:

(current stock price - exercise price) x *number of shares*

Do that separately for vested and non-vested shares. The vested shares are yours to do something with at any time. The non-vested shares are not technically yours until you meet the holding requirements.

Restricted stock is a little more straightforward and is becoming more popular. To value it, you just take the number of shares you have times the current market price. You will owe tax on those shares when the restrictions lapse.

If you are the owner of a business, you probably have contributed money to the firm. List any capital contributions or ownership interests you are sure of receiving on the Net Worth Statement. If the company owes you any money (or you owe the company), list that too.

5. Real Estate
If you own your own home or any other real estate, list the market value. You should also list any associated debt like mortgages or home equity lines of credit (but only if you are actually drawing on your line of credit) as a subtraction.

6. Personal Property
While you aren't going to make any big financial decisions based on your personal property assets, they do make up part of your estate when you die. So list anything you own, like a car or household goods, in this section. You should also list any associated debt as a subtraction.

Sometimes this section can get a little unusual. For example, I have one client who was presented a coffin as a gift once. It's actually a beautiful art piece in itself, so we listed it in the personal property section of his Net Worth Statement. (Now if I can just get him to have his estate documents drawn up!)

7. Life Insurance
We want you to list the value of your life insurance because it's typically a part of your gross estate for estate tax purposes. If you've put your policy in an irrevocable life insurance trust, just footnote it here. That type of trust takes the value of the policy out of your gross estate (assuming it's been at least three years since you transferred the policy to the trust).

8. Bottom Line

Now just add everything up to find out your Net Worth (while you're alive) and your Estimated Total Estate (after your death). Your Estimated Total Estate includes your net life insurance proceeds and is what you use to start to calculate how much your heirs may owe in estate tax.

Are you surprised? Most people don't realize how much it adds up to when you put it all together.

Interpreting Your Net Worth Statement

What I've found over the years is that while many of you have figured out your Net Worth as you applied for loans or completed other forms, most of you have never had a professional give you feedback on how to interpret those numbers. Probably the most valuable part of the process for our clients is gaining insight into where they have done particularly well or where we see problems. We look at factors like balance, liquidity, debt and the potential for happiness! Let's take a moment to do that.

Balance

I seek balance in all things. So it's not surprising that I like to see balance on a Balance Sheet. I look at three broad measures: taxable assets (cash, stocks, bonds), retirement assets and real estate. I like to see some kind of balance among the three groups. An imbalance in a certain area is often a red flag.

For example, sometimes I see new clients who come in with a disproportionate amount of money tied up in real estate. This was especially common a couple of years ago when lots of people purchased second and third properties with the intention of flipping them quickly. As the real estate market all but collapsed in recent years, you can understand why you wouldn't want to be over-concentrated in this one area or really in any area.

Over-concentration is almost always a mistake for most people. While there will always be people like Bill Gates that bet big on one company and profit enormously, that result is rare. Remember instead how that strategy worked for Enron's or WorldCom's employees (not that many of them had a choice). Most of us are better off diversifying our assets and reducing our risk.

Liquidity

Another mistake I see quite often is neglecting to build up taxable assets. Lots of people in their 40s and 50s are doing quite well at building up retirement plan balances and equity in their real estate, but they are "cash poor." It's important to build up a balanced amount of assets in taxable accounts too.

Taxable assets can be valuable in several ways. First of all, they give you freedom. If you decide you want to retire before age 59 ½, you can live on your taxable assets and not have to pay a penalty for tapping retirement accounts too early. Second, it may give you some protection against increases in tax rates.

To the extent that ordinary income tax rates go up, that may mean a bigger burden on retirement account distributions. So to diversify the future tax impact on your assets, you may want to hold more assets in taxable accounts. That's because distributions from taxable accounts are taxed at capital gains rates, which, usually, are more favorable.

Taxable assets are also where your liquidity is held. This typically becomes increasingly important as we get older and enter our retirement years. But it's also important even when we are younger because it can provide peace of mind that should you lose your job or have an unusually large expense, you can handle it financially.

Creating an Emergency Reserve

Your first goal for your taxable assets should be to put an "emergency reserve" in place. An emergency fund is an account where you hold cash that you only tap in the event of an emergency—like losing your job. You want to start by holding at least three months of expenses in this account. By mid-life, you should hold closer to six-months to one-year of expenses. By retirement, you may want to hold several years' worth of expenses in a combination of taxable and retirement accounts.

The higher your income or job level, the more months you should cover with your emergency reserve. It typically takes longer to find those higher level jobs and you may need to cover a longer period of unemployment should you lose your job.

Put your emergency funds in an account that's a little harder to access like a money market or savings account. You want to leave this money alone (unless it's a true emergency!). To avoid touching the emergency funds, keep a small cushion of cash—maybe $2,500 to $10,000—in your checking account (or whatever account you normally use to pay your bills). This cash cushion will keep you from needing to dip into your emergency funds most of the time. It will also help if you have a tendency to overdraw your account.

Debt Obligations

Another aspect to interpreting your Net Worth Statement is analyzing how much debt is appropriate. I know that lots of financial institutions will encourage you to leverage your assets to take on more debt. I'm not saying that can't be a good scenario at times, but it has gotten out of hand. I see lots of people who think they can charge whatever they want on credit cards with no regard to their ability to pay it back in a timely manner. This can lead to serious problems with credit ratings or even future bankruptcy. Part of finding financial happiness is figuring out how to deal with debt. That may not be easy, but it is essential.

Let's focus on a simple ratio you can use to assess whether it's prudent to take on any more debt. The "debt-to-income" ratio allows you to see how much of your cash flow is going toward paying off debt obligations. If you over-commit to how much you are going to pay every month, you may find yourself getting frustrated that you can't enjoy many of the things in life that come along that you'd like to participate in. You know, the fun things like going to a concert, or joining a health club, or going out to eat now and then.

Probably the first time you came face-to-face with the "debt-to-income ratio" was when you were trying to buy a house. The mortgage industry rule of thumb is to keep home-related debt expenses (principal + interest + real estate tax + homeowners' insurance) below 28% of your pre-tax income, or to keep total debt below 36% (all debt divided by pre-tax income).

I think those ratios are too high. To give yourself a margin of safety, knock off 6% and use 22% for home-related debt and 30% for all debt. So if you make $109,000 in income annually, you can afford approximately $2,000 a month for mortgage payments plus real estate tax plus homeowners' insurance. And you shouldn't have more than $725 a month in additional types of debt payments like credit card bills, car loans or student loans.

If that feels restrictive to you, you've probably bought into the rampant consumerism culture that encourages all of us to overspend. But in the long run, this kind of behavior becomes unsustainable. We need to be building assets and managing our spending. It's so easy to get into the habit of buying what you want because it feels better right now.

Happiness

Remember, the goal here is to put your money where your heart is. And to stack the odds in your favor, you don't want to get so bogged down in debt that you don't have enough breathing room. So even though you may be temporarily disappointed that you can't afford more, you will find that your life has more freedom because you didn't over-commit on your debt obligations. You will also be forced to find other ways to entertain yourself that don't cost a lot. And that may be one of the secrets of finding true happiness.

Having balance and liquidity in your financial picture will also help protect you from whatever life throws at you next. It's much easier to recover from financial setbacks when you haven't taken on too much risk and you have a financial cushion. And as we all get older, this becomes more and more important to our well-being.

Net Worth Stories

One of the best ways to learn is to observe lots of different situations to see what works and what doesn't. So let's take a look at three different cases. These are based on real people, but I've changed anything that could identify them. Stories may also represent a composite of several clients with the same goals and outcomes.

Lisa's Negative Liquidity

Lisa has had a number of financial setbacks in her life and it shows on her Net Worth Statement. To me, this only means that from here things are going to get much better. Think how good it will be for her to look back in ten years and see how her life (and her Net Worth Statement) has improved!

But that won't happen without some effort. I know it's sometimes easier to bury your head in the sand than to face the facts, but I promise it's worth the effort as you see your situation improve.

As I wrote earlier, we typically see negative net worth values with younger people, but Lisa is in her 40s. Let's take a look at her Statement and then I'll comment on what Lisa should do to improve her situation.

Lisa Net Worth Statement		
	Lisa	Total By Category
ASSETS		
Taxable Accounts		-$11,400
Cash		-$14,900
Checking	$10,000	
Merrill Lynch Money Market	100	
Savings	5,000	
Less: Credit Card Debt	-30,000	
Fixed Income		$1,000
Savings Bond	$1,000	
Equities		$2,500
Merrill Lynch Stocks	$2,500	
Retirement Accounts		$3,500
Fidelity IRA	$3,500	
Real Estate		$0
Personal Property		$4,500
Furniture and Household Goods	$1,500	
Jewelry	1,000	
Automobiles	10,000	
Less: Loan	-8,000	
Other Collectibles	0	
NET WORTH	-$3,400	-$3,400
Life Insurance Death Benefit	$0	$0
ESTIMATED TOTAL ESTATE	-$3,400	-$3,400

Credit card debt is the culprit here. It's causing the negative liquidity and Lisa needs a plan to deal with it. She's completely out of balance. Her first step is to look at the interest rates she pays on the five credit cards she holds balances on and start paying them off, starting with the highest rate. We were able to talk about some expenses she could temporarily cut back on to find the additional cash to get all of her debt paid off over the next year. Even small things like stretching out the time between haircuts can help when you're trying to cut expenses. Of course, in this case it's going to take more than that.

But paying off existing balances is never the complete answer. Lisa needs to make sure she never gets herself in this position again. There are two things I recommend to help ensure this: getting her emergency reserves in place and keeping close tabs on what she charges. This will help ensure that Lisa builds up her liquidity. So as Lisa is paying more per month to reduce her credit card debt, she'll also need to be saving money to build-up her emergency reserves. And she can use the debt-to-income ratio to make sure she can afford to charge something going forward.

In the short-term, this will probably mean that Lisa shouldn't charge much until her debt levels are lower. She'll need to pay cash or make sure she can pay off a credit card balance immediately. I know how easy it is to fall into the trap of charging now and worrying about it later. I've done it too. But you aren't really going to be in control of your financial life until you get a grip on this. Even if you have lots of cash flow and feel like you should be able to cover most of your credit card monthly expenses, be careful of letting your money slip through your hands with careless charge card habits.

Once Lisa has her credit card debt under control and an emergency reserve in place, she can continue to build up her other assets. She can contribute $5,000 a year to an IRA and she should also try to save $5,000 a year in her taxable accounts. Over time she will accumulate enough liquid assets to eventually put a down-payment on a home if she decides that is what will make her happy. Or perhaps she'd rather rent and use the incremental difference toward something else that matters to her.

Finally, Lisa will need to do some catching-up in accumulating assets if she wants to retire before she's 70. While she's still young enough to accumulate a healthy retirement nest egg, she'll likely have to make some trade-offs. If she has meaningful work that she enjoys, working longer may be acceptable to her. If she can live on less, she may be able to find a balance of part-time work and part-time leisure that gives her fulfillment.

Susan's Post-Divorce Transformation

Susan came to us in 2004 shortly after her divorce from a prominent doctor. She was used to a life of luxury and was now very concerned about her future. She had been granted a reasonable divorce settlement, but really knew nothing about how to start her new life financially.

Five years later, Susan is happy, has a job she loves and is dating a wonderful new man. She found a townhouse that she could afford and that has given her the confidence that she can succeed on her own. Let's take a look at her Net Worth Statement in 2004 and in 2009 to see how her life has changed *(see page 34)*.

Overall, you can see that Susan has increased her estimated total estate by $134,500 since we started working together. She's also found more balance in her financial life: how her wealth is distributed is important to note.

She started out in 2004 with almost $500,000 in cash, but no marketable assets and no home. So in this case, there was plenty of liquidity—in fact, too much liquidity. As of 2009, she now has a more appropriate amount of liquidity ($37,300) and has $430,000 invested in stocks and bonds.

She also owns a $360,000 townhouse with $88,000 in mortgage debt. This is a perfectly reasonable level of debt. But one of her goals is to have that paid off by the time her alimony stops in three years. Having no debt will give her a sense of freedom and flexibility.

Susan will also have some catch-up work to do on her retirement planning. Her $450,000 in retirement accounts won't be enough to provide sufficient cash flow to last through her lifetime with her projected expenses. So we will be actively working on finding creative solutions that allow her to build a satisfying life that she enjoys which can also support her financial needs. These include aggressive savings while she is receiving alimony, finding a lifestyle that she loves and can afford well into her retirement years and investing for conservative growth and eventually income.

Susan
Net Worth Statement

	2004	Total By Category	% of Assets	2009	Total By Category	% of Assets
ASSETS						
Taxable Accounts		$490,000	48%		$471,200	36%
Cash		$490,000			$37,300	
Chase Checking	$3,000			$3,000		
Chase CD 5.25% (6-month)	0			10,000		
Harris Savings	308,000			13,300		
Schwab Cash	67,500			11,000		
Schwab US Treasury Money Fund	60,000			0		
Receivable: Divorce Settlement	51,500			0		
Fixed Income		$0			$168,300	
Schwab Bonds	$0			$168,300		
Equities		$0			$265,600	
Schwab	$0			$265,600		
Retirement Accounts		$414,400	40%		$447,200	35%
Defined Benefit Plan	$131,000			$0		
Fidelity IRA	273,800			0		
Merrill Lynch IRA	9,600			0		
Schwab IRA	0			447,200		
Limited Partnerships		$17,500	2%		$0	0%
XYZ Partners	$17,500			$0		
Real Estate		$0	0%		$272,000	21%
Personal Residence	$0			$360,000		
Less: Mortgage	0			-88,000		
Personal Property		$102,000	10%		$102,000	8%
Art and Antiques	$5,000			$10,000		
Automobiles	30,000			25,000		
Furniture and Household Goods	50,000			50,000		
Jewelry	17,000			17,000		
NET WORTH	$1,023,900	$1,023,900	100%	$1,292,400	$1,292,400	100%
Life Insurance Death Benefit		$200,000			$66,000	
Employer Sponsored Term	$200,000			$66,000		
ESTIMATED TOTAL ESTATE	$1,223,900	$1,223,900	100%	$1,358,400	$1,358,400	100%

Mike and Lisa's Windfall

Mike and Lisa are a couple in their 40s who wound up with more money than they could have imagined. He works for a smaller company that went public in 2005. He got in on the ground floor of the business and cashed in on about $10 million in stock options over the past three years *(see page 36)*.

Their net worth is over $18 million, and when you factor in life insurance, it's almost $20 million. They never expected this. They know their kids' college is covered, the house is paid off and neither really needs to work for the rest of their lives, although they want to. So liquidity and debt obligations are in good shape here.

Balance is the problem. Their biggest challenge is to convert the concentrated company stock to a more diversified portfolio of assets over the next five years. At this time they don't need income from their assets, but we have positioned them for that going forward. They have a sizeable municipal bond portfolio, and are reinvesting the interest it produces, but should they decide to take income from the portfolio, we can always have the bond income paid out to them. They also want to create a portfolio that is socially conscious and allows them to do charitable giving going forward. This is something they find rewarding and that makes them happy, and is clearly a good example of Putting Your Money Where Your Heart Is.

Although their taxable assets will provide plenty of capital for them throughout their lifetimes, they are still contributing the maximum allowed to both their 401(k) plans. Tax management will be a big issue for Mike and Lisa—including ordinary income tax, capital gains tax and estate tax. As tax laws change going forward, they will need to be aware of everything they can do to make sure they preserve their wealth.

Because of the limits on contributions to retirement accounts (such as employer-sponsored plans and IRAs), real estate may offer Mike and Lisa additional opportunity to diversify their assets. With property values at lower valuations currently, this may offer an interesting opportunity—especially since they would not need to take on debt to finance a purchase. We will carefully evaluate whether this type of asset makes sense financially and also might be something that their whole family could enjoy for many years.

Mike & Lisa
Net Worth Statement

	Mike	Lisa	Joint	Total	Total by Category	% of Assets
ASSETS						
Taxable Accounts					$5,045,500	27%
Cash					$45,500	
Northern Trust	$10,000	$7,500	$25,000	$42,500		
Schwab Money Market	2,000	1,000	0	3,000		
Fixed Income					$2,200,000	
Municipal Bonds	$1,000,000	$1,200,000	$0	$2,200,000		
Equities					$2,800,000	
Schwab Equity Funds	$0	$2,800,000	$0	$2,800,000		
Retirement Accounts					$650,000	4%
Company 401(k)	$50,000	$500,000	$0	$550,000		
Schwab IRA	50,000	50,000	0	100,000		
Company Accounts					$11,925,000	64%
Company Stock	$2,500,000	$0	$0	$2,500,000		
Non-Qualified Stock Options (vested)	6,000,000	0	0	6,000,000		
Non-Qualified Stock Options (non-vested)	3,000,000	0	0	3,000,000		
Restricted Stock	425,000	0	0	425,000		
Real Estate					$1,000,000	5%
Personal Residence	$0	$0	$1,000,000	$1,000,000		
Personal Property					$75,000	0%
Automobiles	$0	$0	$20,000	$20,000		
Furniture and Household Goods	0	0	50,000	50,000		
Jewelry	0	0	5,000	5,000		
NET WORTH	**$13,037,000**	**$4,558,500**	**$1,100,000**	**$18,695,500**	**$18,695,500**	**100%**
Life Insurance Death Benefit					$1,150,000	
Employer Sponsored	$150,000	$300,000	$0	$450,000		
Term	400,000	300,000	0	700,000		
ESTIMATED TOTAL ESTATE	**$13,587,000**	**$5,158,500**	**$1,100,000**	**$19,845,500**		

Summary

As you can see in each of these three scenarios, no matter how the numbers are distributed, there are a whole set of issues that need to be addressed. The amount of money you have doesn't mean you won't have concerns. It's just that the types of concerns vary with different levels of wealth. And I can tell you that it's possible to find financial happiness in any of these situations.

As you work through your own Net Worth Statement, keep these concepts in mind:

1. Don't guess where you stand financially—know what you owe and what you own.
2. Understand what the numbers are telling you—reflect on balance, liquidity and debt obligations as you interpret your Statement.

In the next chapter you'll focus on how to invest your money. This is a source of worry and frustration for many people. It doesn't have to be that way. It is possible to balance risk and reward and ultimately find Portfolio Peace of Mind™.

Chapter 4

Portfolio Peace of Mind™

A Fresh Approach to Money Management

"Wealth is the ability to fully experience life."
~ Henry David Thoreau

When you stop and think about it, what most people really want from their portfolio is peace of mind. To be able to sleep at night without excessive worry. To know their hard-earned money is working for them and that they have the right balance between risk and reward.

The topic of money is almost always highly charged. That's because money is not only a financial currency, it's an emotional currency. People want some sense of security about where they stand today and how they will survive in the future.

The topic of investing is expansive. It could easily take up a whole book—and has. We are going to focus on three things in this chapter:

» Balancing Risk and Reward
» Creating a Disciplined Approach
» Aligning Your Values

Balancing Risk and Reward

Ultimately investing comes down to finding the right balance of risk and reward for who you are at this point in your life. It's like having one foot on the risk side of a teeter-totter and the other foot on reward. By shifting your weight, you find the right balance. Different combinations of risk and reward are appropriate for different times in your life and varying circumstances.

Time and time again, I see prospective new clients who haven't yet found the right balance. They put too much money in technology stocks in the late 1990s. Or they invested too much in real estate before the bubble burst. Or they thought the stock market could never go down—not THAT much.

Most of the things that trip people up are a question of balance. Let's take a closer look at what I've found to be the biggest pitfalls to an investment strategy that lets you get a good night's sleep:

The Top Ten Pitfalls for Portfolio Peace of Mind™

1. Being Overly Aggressive
If you are looking for a smoother ride in the stock market, take a look at your asset allocation–your mix of stocks and bonds. This is how you balance risk and reward. Don't take more risk than you need to. Once you have analyzed your portfolio from this broader perspective, you can move on to examining each of your individual holdings to see if they are aligned with your overall goals of consistency and steady performance.

2. Investing Too Narrowly
In the search for a low-anxiety portfolio, one of your best bets is to spread your assets (and your risk) to a wide variety of investments. You should start with "core" holdings in the major asset classes to anchor your investment line-up. Broad-based index funds and exchange-traded funds are

prototypical core investments–even the most sophisticated pension fund and endowment managers use them as such. Each goal you have identified should be supported by a group of core funds–think of them as your portfolio's foundation. They are primarily responsible for achieving your objectives. Core funds typically cover large-cap domestic and foreign stocks, taxable and tax-exempt bonds.

Once your core is built, it's fine to seek a bit more diversification, but it's also easy to go too far. Adding exposure to asset classes like mid- and small-cap stocks, emerging market stocks and alternative assets can provide a useful dose of diversification to your portfolio, but it's important to keep them in check. These asset classes are historically much more volatile, and investors are most likely to fall in love with them only after they've provided spectacular short-term performance–just in time, in many instances, to catch the downside.

3. Being An Under-Informed Investor

Part of finding peace of mind is knowing what to expect. You can't do that unless you've taken the time to educate yourself about the financial markets. Step Two of our Comprehensive Process is all about The Fundamentals of Finance. You'll read more about that shortly.

Find some way to continue learning about personal finance. Perhaps a subscription to *The Wall Street Journal* or *Radiant Wealth* (www.financial-happiness.com). See Appendix C for a list of books I've found to be helpful.

4. Being Undisciplined and Overly Emotional

Don't fall in love with your investments. You need to have discipline and set your expectations. The best way I know to do that is through an Investment Policy Statement (IPS). Creating an Investment Policy Statement is a great way to establish beforehand how you'll deal with the inevitable tough questions, and minimize the impact of emotions.

You'll need to think about questions like: What is my risk tolerance? What range of returns should I expect? Which asset classes should I choose and how much should I allocate per asset class? What risk reduction techniques will I use? Thinking through questions such as these is the difference between having a cohesive investment program and just a collection of funds and/or individual securities.

5. Being Impatient

Peace of mind comes with patience. One thing I've learned over the years is to not react too quickly to market conditions. It's tempting though, isn't it? Sometimes you just want to do something when you're feeling anxious.

One of the best ways I've found to avoid doing this is to simply try to tune out the noise about the market's day-to-day gyrations. Once you have your portfolio in place, you'll be far better served by ignoring the screaming and shouting on CNBC, which will help you avoid jumping in or out of the market and learn to persevere through the inevitable market drops. Stick to the discipline of your IPS.

6. Getting Greedy

Did your folks ever tell you to keep your eye on the ball? That was good advice. When times are good, lots of people get distracted by the "high" of making money and lose sight of their true goals. They fall into the trap of always wanting more. There's a famous story of Kurt Vonnegut talking with Joseph Heller while at a party thrown by a billionaire. Kurt commented on the wealth of their host, and Joe Heller responded that he had something their host never would. "Enough." That's the title of one of Jack Bogle's latest books, which is well worth a read.

If you're meeting your objectives, don't get greedy and think the grass is greener by taking on unnecessary risk. The vast majority of the time, it's just not worth it.

7. Ignoring Tax Efficiency

There are differing opinions on where you should hold your stock and bond investments. Some feel that it's better to own stocks in taxable accounts (thus taking advantage of the current low tax rates on dividends and long-term capital gains) and bonds in tax-deferred accounts (thus shielding the income they provide that would otherwise be taxed at ordinary income tax rates). Others feel that stocks, particularly stock mutual funds, are best held in tax-deferred accounts to maximize their long-term growth. This discussion of where to hold assets for tax advantage is known as "asset location."

The reality is that what's best for you depends on where you hold the bulk of your assets, your personal tax situation, and how willing and able you are to make adjustments based upon tax law changes. Once you've set your asset allocation and your Investment Policy, go back over the types of assets you hold (taxable and tax-deferred) and think about where you might have a tax advantage. For example, if you are in a high tax bracket, you may want to hold municipal bonds that aren't taxed federally (and sometimes state too) in taxable accounts. You'll also need to give thought to the tax effect of what you plan to sell. With some planning, you may be able to net out capital gains and losses (perhaps over several years) and pay less tax.

8. Paying Too Much

Other than perhaps your asset allocation, nothing will impact your total long-term growth more than the fees you pay. It's really quite simple–the more you pay, the less you keep. Even seemingly small differences in annual expenses can have a dramatic impact. For example, let's say that you invest $10,000 in a fund with annual expenses of 0.5 percent, and your friend chooses one with expenses of 2 percent. If you each earn an annual return of 8 percent before expenses for 40 years, your final balance will be $180,400. Your friend's total? $102,900, or just 57 percent of yours. Yes, costs matter. If anyone tells you any differently, smile politely and make a mental note to never take any investment advice from them.

9. Rebalancing Too Often or Too Little

Even the most finely tuned portfolios will see their asset allocation drift over time, as some asset classes do better than others. While relatively minor changes (plus or minus a few percentage points or so) aren't necessarily worrisome, it is possible that your allocation has shifted dramatically if you haven't given it much attention over the past several years. If that's the case, you might be taking on more risk than you intend.

Recent studies show that the optimal time between portfolio rebalancing may be as long as six years. Now some people are going to get very nervous waiting that long, so we'd recommend that you try to limit any major rebalancing to once a year. If you find yourself out of alignment you may want to dollar cost average (systematically moving money over a longer period of time) back to your target allocation.

When rebalancing your portfolio, consider the type of accounts you hold. If you invest primarily in tax-deferred accounts, you can rebalance back to your original allocation without any harmful tax consequences. If, on the other hand, you need to rebalance assets that have appreciated in a taxable account, you should try to bring your portfolio into balance by investing new money in underweighted asset classes instead of selling something else.

10. Forgetting to Put Your Money Where Your Heart Is!

Finally, one of the most important rules of finding portfolio peace of mind is to choose investments that reflect your own personal ideals. This connection to what your money is invested in will help you through the hard times.

For example, let's say you love music. Perhaps you can build in a special category for music when you do your budgeting. As your portfolio grows, perhaps you take a certain percentage of profits to use to enjoy concerts. Or if your profits allow, to contribute to an arts organization. Because you are using your money to enjoy life, you will find the inspiration to save and invest even more money in the future. It's a self-fulfilling prophesy.

Your money needs to work hard for you to achieve the things you want in life. There is much you cannot control, but by following these guidelines you'll avoid many of the pitfalls and move closer to attaining Portfolio Peace of Mind™.

A Few More Words About Risk

Fear of risk prevents a lot of people from moving forward—in life as well as investing. But for almost every kind of financial risk out there, there is a way to manage that risk. Let's take a closer look at ten of the most prevalent risks:

1. Cash

Although cash types of accounts like money markets, checking and savings accounts, even short-term CDs (certificates of deposit) are generally quite stable, they aren't entirely "safe."

In the case of a money market, it is possible that the dollar you put in could be worth less coming out. It's rare, but it has happened. (In fact it happened recently in the fall of 2008.) That's called "breaking the buck." Bank deposits, like checking, savings and CDs, can be at risk if the bank has credit problems and goes into default.

The Emergency Economic Stabilization Act of 2008 increased the FDIC (Federal Deposit Insurance Corporation) coverage of bank deposits to $250,000. So even if your bank failed, you still would be protected up to the limits of this coverage assuming your account was FDIC insured. This program is in place through 2013.

If you have cash in brokerage accounts, SIPC (Securities Investor Protection Corporation) covers up to $100,000 in sweep types of money market accounts. Position-traded money markets are typically considered a "security" and are covered up to $500,000 (but check with your brokerage to be sure you understand their definitions of coverage).

An often-overlooked risk associated with cash accounts is the risk of inflation. It's possible–indeed, perhaps probable–that the interest you earn in a money market or savings account will not keep up with annual inflation, meaning that your money will have less buying power when you take it out than it did when you put it in.

In deflationary times, holding cash can be beneficial. Prices drop and your dollar buys more. Holding some cash can also be a good strategy if you expect stock markets to drop, offering unusually good buying opportunities.

2. Bonds

There are several types of risk that relate to bond, or fixed-income, investments. First, if the underlying issuing entity faces default, you can lose a part or all of your investment. One of the ways to manage default risk is to look at the ratings given to bonds by credit rating agencies like S&P or Moody's or purchase bonds that have been insured. Unfortunately neither is fool-proof. Ratings agencies have been known to get it wrong and bond insurers can be financially unstable themselves. We've seen both in the recent past.

Typically bond-holders are in line in front of stock-holders in the event of a default–but that still doesn't mean you'll get all of your money back. In the past year, we've seen the government step in and take over companies in distress. In these cases, a new class of ownership can be created that could step in front of bond owners. That could set a dangerous new precedent. To lessen this risk with any one security, hold at least a portion of your bonds in mutual funds.

Bonds are also affected by interest rates. When rates go down, the value of bonds typically goes up (and vice versa). So if you want to sell your bond before it matures, you might get less for it in the secondary market if a new bond now offers a higher interest rate. To protect against the risk of rising interest rates when you are invested in bonds, keep the maturity short. The shorter the maturity, the less volatility typically.

Keep in mind, lower-risk bonds pay less interest. But many people feel they want to take more risk in the stock market and keep their bonds less risky. If so, choose primarily high-quality bonds with little chance for loss of principal.

3. Stocks

September and October 2008 were historic examples of extreme risk (volatility) in the stock market. As of March 2009, we saw both the total U.S. and foreign stock markets plunge about 55% from the market highs in October 2007. The best way to manage risk in the stock market is to limit how much you put there. You can also choose less risky stocks, but even many traditionally strong dividend-paying stocks have been hit hard in the recession.

"Bubbles" are another risk in the stock market. When too many speculators rush into a specific asset class it artificially pushes up the price–temporarily. That's what we saw in the late 1990s when investors couldn't get enough of technology stocks. But that all ended with the bear market that started in March 2000.

Manage the risk of stocks by creating a balanced portfolio. And diversify the types of stocks you hold to spread the risk across multiple asset classes.

4. Foreign Stocks

Not only do you have volatility in foreign stocks, you also have currency risk. When the dollar strengthens, the value of your foreign investment goes down (and vice versa). You can purchase "hedged" foreign stock mutual funds, but you lose the diversification value that unhedged investments add. The best way to manage this risk is to keep the percentage you invest in proportion to your risk tolerance.

5. Regulatory Risks

We've seen a whole host of new regulatory and tax law changes in recent years (including the Emergency Economic Stabilization Act). Every time we get "new rules," it means we need to take a fresh look at our portfolios to see if we need to adjust anything. And you can bet more change is coming.

6. Longevity Risk

No one wants to outlive their money. So you have to make sure that you are periodically re-assessing the adequacy of your accumulated assets. Depending on market conditions, that may mean making a change to the amount you are withdrawing from your portfolio or how you are allocating your assets.

7. Inflation

One of the biggest risks facing any economy is inflation–when the value of your dollar buys less. There are types of assets you can purchase, like TIPS (Treasury Inflation-Protected Securities) or I-Bonds (a type of U.S. Savings Bond), that have a portion of their total return that moves in step with inflation. You can also purchase inflation riders on some types of investments like annuities.

8. Human Capital

Your ability to work lessens the risk that your portfolio won't be able to support you throughout life. There is always a risk that you could lose your job or be unable to work due to disability. Unemployment and disability insurance can help mitigate these risks. But most people need to decrease the risk levels in their asset mix to help protect against loss of income as they get older.

9. Geopolitical Risk

Whenever we have a large-scale war, or terrorist event, it affects world financial markets. To some extent, holding a little less in stocks or adding hard assets like precious metals may help mitigate any sudden drop due to turmoil in the U.S. or around the globe. But realistically, there is very little you can do to protect against these catastrophic unexpected events. All the more reason to put your money where your heart is right now.

10. Time Horizon

The closer you get to your goal, the more you need to protect your accumulated assets. A classic example is college funding. You don't want to experience a strong market drop right before you need to draw out the money. So keep an eye on the end date for your goal and adjust your portfolio so you know you'll have what you need when you need it.

Risk is one part of the equation. For every kind of risk, there is a way to help manage that risk, although it's doubtful you can completely eliminate risk.

And Let's Not Forget Reward

If you take risk, you expect to be rewarded. But it's not always true that the more risk you take, the greater the reward. There has to be a balance. At some point, too much risk can have disastrous results.

And let's get one thing clear: putting your money where your heart is does not necessarily mean putting all your money in something you have a strong emotional tie to. Just because I love to shop at Whole Foods (yes, I know it's expensive), does not mean I should run out and put all my money in that stock.

Putting your money where your heart is requires an intelligent, disciplined approach. That will give you the best chance at building assets that will give you the freedom to do what you want to and to reward those entities that are doing work you respect and admire.

It also means taking a second look at how you define reward. Reward can be looking at your brokerage statement and smiling because you like the results. Or reward can be writing the check that pays for your child's college education—that satisfaction that comes from meeting your goal. Reward will mean different things to different people.

Reward brings happiness. It may be quite simple, but it has an emotional connection. It does not always mean that you have a million dollar portfolio. It may not mean that you have the highest returns on your investments. But you should expect a reasonable return for the risk you are taking.

Sometimes we forget to celebrate our achievements. We get caught up in the pursuit of "more." That's why we like to review how far we've come each year as we complete Step One of our disciplined process that we'll share next.

No matter how much money you have, it doesn't guarantee happiness. Happiness comes from within. As an advisor, I have had a uniquely intimate view into the lives of many very successful people. And what I've observed is that having more money does not necessarily correlate with having more happiness. We just have to look at the experience of lottery winners or trust fund babies to know that sudden wealth brings with it a whole host of problems.

Enjoying your wealth happens from a shift in attitude. It's colored by the way you view the world. It's a head game you can win through your heart.

Happiness is determined more by one's state of mind than by external events....Our moment-to-moment happiness is largely determined by our outlook. In fact, whether we are feeling happy or unhappy at any given moment often has very little to do with our absolute convictions but, rather it is a function of how we perceive our situation, how satisfied we are with what we have.

Let us reflect on what is truly of value in life, what gives meaning to our lives, and set our priorities on the basis of that. The purpose of our life needs to be positive... For our life to be of value, I think we must develop basic good human qualities—warmth, kindness, compassion. Then our life becomes meaningful and more peaceful—happier.

~ His Holiness The Dalai Lama

Creating a Disciplined Approach

If you've been conscious at all in the past few years, you know that investing can be a roller coaster of ups and downs. Even the steadiest hand can shake when facing extreme volatility. So it helps to have a plan that you create in advance for what to do. We've done just that—a six-step process that works.

The Stevens Wealth Management (SWM) Comprehensive Investment Process

After many years of managing money, I've seen what works and what doesn't. Chasing hot stocks gets you burned. I learned about discipline playing the cello. Practice does make perfect. The same principles apply to finance.

Having discipline means taking much of the fear and emotion out of the money management equation. If you concentrate on following the steps outlined below, you'll avoid many of the amateur mistakes almost everybody makes.

The Stevens Wealth Management (SWM) Comprehensive Investment Process is a six-step process for reviewing and managing your portfolio. Following this structured approach greatly increases your chance for investment success and ultimately Portfolio Peace of Mind™.

Step One: The Independent Portfolio Assessment

Start where you are. Use what you have. Do what you can.
~ Arthur Ashe

To paraphrase a line from Groundhog's Day, "This first step is a doozy." I realize this step takes up a great deal of this chapter, but it's that important. I've developed this assessment over many years of practice. We use it as we prepare for our Stevens Wealth Management clients' annual reviews. I've honed the questions down to what I feel are the most important issues to focus on year-after-year. Now you can use this at home to take a comprehensive look at how your investments integrate with the rest of your personal finance matters.

This portfolio check-up offers not only a detailed look at your current portfolio, but also incorporates other financial considerations in your life. It all needs to work together to create a cohesive plan. It covers how your assets have grown, if your portfolio performance is on track with your expectations, if you need to adjust your asset allocation, what your tax return is telling you, how your retirement plans are shaping up, if you've missed anything important in planning your estate and so forth.

Step One of this process is where you conceptualize how to put your money where your heart is. The other steps implement your decisions and complete the process. You can see *The Independent Portfolio Assessment* in its entirety in Appendix A. This chapter will break it down section-by-section to help you understand how to fill it out and use it to think about your present challenges and future opportunities.

Completing The Independent Portfolio Assessment

I'll break the checklist down by section and show you how to enter your own information. We've used a hypothetical example to help you visualize the end result.

Part 1: What Are You Trying To Do?

***Your Name	Age:***	*Mary age 47*
***Your Spouse's Name	Age:***	*Antonio age 53*
***Your Children's Names	Ages:***	*Ryan age 10, Emma age 9*
Your Parent's Names	*Joe 72, Beth 68, Juan 75, Pia 74*

This is very basic, but I still like to think about how old each client is every year. And not only the client (you, in this case), but the children and parents. Families often come as a package deal and one part affects the whole.

Thinking about age helps put planning in context—at least to some extent. For example, if you are in your mid-50s and you've been considering retirement in your late 50s or early 60s, you may want to start running annual projections to see how realistic those plans are. And in light of market conditions in 2008-2009, that's even more important. In most cases, you're going to have to increase your savings or modify your expectations to stay on course.

Of course age doesn't always drive financial decisions. Some of you have already accumulated a significant amount of money earlier in life and choose to treat it more conservatively (like a retirement nest egg) so that you have the freedom to tap the income and know that you have more flexibility in your decisions.

Age matters with kids too. As your kids get older, you have to think about the issues that affect them. As they reach college age, you generally need to get more conservative with their assets. When they reach the age of majority, you need to change their custodial accounts to their own names.

Depending on your parents' circumstances, you may need to have a conversation with them about elder care. Do they have adequate financial resources? Will they need assisted living? It's not always easy to initiate these conversations, but it's better to try before a problem arises. Thinking about how old they are periodically helps remind you that they may need your help at some point—even if that's just moral support for the aging process.

What Matters Most (Where Your Heart Is)
Creating happy family memories, providing a quality education, staying healthy,
participating in the community, looking forward to work because it makes a difference,
enjoying life, sharing my wealth with others

Long-Term Objectives as of: *January 2010*
Save for kids' college funding, save for retirement and possibly to help our parents,
save for a new car in two years, accumulate enough savings that I could consider
opening my own business in five-to-ten years

Next Year's Objectives
Increase emergency savings to cover eight months of expenses, save $500 a month,
set up automatic savings deposits from checking to investment account, increase company
retirement savings, take community college class on business interest, talk to parents about
their retirement security, set aside one hour a week to work on personal finance

Setting your intention is critical. If you don't know what you want your money to do, you won't be able to evaluate whether you've been successful. Are you trying to get your debt under control? Have you set up how much to pay each month to make that happen within a certain amount of time? Are you keeping your current spending under control so the problem doesn't escalate? Try to choose a couple of key focal points so that you have a good chance of meeting your goals as soon as is realistically possible.

Net Worth Statement

| *Net Worth (Inception)* | *$350,000* | *Date: 1/1/2003* |
| *Net Worth (Current)* | *$500,000* | *Date: 1/1/2010* |

- ✓ Is the level of emergency reserves adequate?
- ✓ Is the level of debt reasonable?
- ✓ Look at debt/income ratio
- ✓ Can you restructure the debt?
- ✓ Is there balance?

We talked about creating your Net Worth Statement (NWS) in Chapter Three. I always find it enlightening to see how the current NWS compares to the very first one you complete. Typically, you should see your assets grow and your liabilities decrease over time. But every now and then, you may have setbacks. 2008 is a good example of seeing asset values decrease in financial accounts and in real estate too.

Apply what you've learned in Chapter Three: Is your debt reasonable? Is your debt-to-income ratio acceptable? Do you have enough liquidity? Should you restructure your debt? Is your overall financial picture balanced?

Credit

| *Credit Report Reviewed* | *Date: 1/15/2010* |

While you're thinking about issues concerning debt, when is the last time you checked your credit report? You should do that about once a year. It's free at www.annualcreditreport.com. When you get the report, look for anything that you know is not true. For example, when I looked at mine several years ago, I saw a mortgage for "Fred Stevens." I don't know any Fred Stevens and I sure didn't want his mortgage on my credit report. So I wrote the credit agencies a letter and they took it off of my record. Now when I review the annual updates, everything looks accurate.

PART 2: A Close-Up for Your Portfolio

Portfolio Details

Current Date: January 2010

Asset Class	Current Allocation	IPS	Revised IPS
Cash	3%	0-5%	0-10%
Domestic Fixed Income*	20%	30%	40-50%
Intl Fixed Income	0%	0%	0-5%
Large-Cap Stock*	40%	40-50%	10-25%
Mid-Small-Cap Stock	27%	10-25%	5-15%
Intl Stock	10%	5-10%	5-20%
Alternative	0%	0-5%	0-10%
Other	0%	0%	0%

Balanced funds are split 50/50 between fixed income and large-cap stocks

Portfolio Specifics	Data
Total Return Prior Year:	-25%
Total Return Most Recent Quarter:	+8%
Total Return Since Inception:	+6%
Inception Date:	1/1/2005
Risk Tolerance:	Conservative-to-moderate
Expected Return Range:	5-7%
Current Liquidity Reserve :	$10,000
Last Rebalance Date:	1/1/2008

Now it's time to do some diagnostics on your portfolio. It's like the nurse taking your vital signs before you see the doctor. Take a moment to collect a few important statistics about your investments.

Your mix of stocks, bonds and cash is critical. It drives risk and reward. Your Investment Policy Statement (IPS) is the document that captures your objectives for investing and sets up the parameters. If you've done this type of analysis in the past, you can fill out the current IPS section.

The first column sets out your current mix of stocks, bonds and cash. It is further broken down by sub-asset class. To see how your portfolio splits out into these various sectors, enter your holdings in the Portfolio Manager tool at www.morningstar.com. The X-Ray feature is particularly helpful. You can also enter the tickers of your holdings in the free Quotes box on the site to see what category each investment falls in.

The second column is your current IPS for the portfolio. This is your strategic asset allocation—the long-term mix of asset classes that you keep relatively stable for a particular investment goal. You'll see in my example that I often use ranges of expected returns. Later in this chapter I'll discuss tactical asset allocation. These ranges give you some latitude as to where you want to be within any sub-asset class.

The third column shows what changes you expect to make to your IPS at this time. You may find that your current target asset allocation mix does not need to change. However, from time to time, you may want to tweak the target ranges as your circumstances change.

The other Portfolio Specifics help you check up on your portfolio's health. How did your portfolio do last year? Last quarter? Don't be afraid to look. You can find this type of information on many custodial websites. You need to know so that you can get back on track. Compare return data to your expectations of performance that are set out in your IPS.

Jot down how much money you plan to hold in cash reserves. This is your emergency fund. You should have at least six months of expenses in a liquid account like a money market or Certificate of Deposit (CD).

PART 3: How Do Other Aspects of Personal Finance Affect Investment Decisions?

We like to look at other major areas of planning like taxes, retirement planning, college funding and estate planning as we work through our comprehensive annual investment review. Each of these areas may have implications for how you invest.

Tax Return	Date: 2008
Adjusted Gross Income (p.1):	$65,000
Taxable Income (p.2):	$35,000
Year-to-Date Realized Gains/Losses:	-$5,000
Loss Carry-forwards (Schedule D):	-$10,000
Marginal Tax Rate:	25%
Effective Tax Rate:	17%

    ✓ Is the portfolio tax-efficient?

    ✓ Review asset location

You should understand a few basics about your tax return. One important number is AGI: Adjusted Gross Income. It's at the bottom of page 1 of your federal 1040 return. It's important because your eligibility for certain tax breaks keys off that number.

Taxable Income is found on page 2 of your return. This is what the government uses as a basis for assessing your tax. It's all of your earnings less deductions. Most people don't know the difference between AGI and Taxable Income, but it's relevant as you plan your investment and retirement strategies.

We always pay attention to realized gains and losses. After 2008, you should pay particular attention to "loss carry forwards" on Schedule D. You can use $3,000 of capital losses a year to offset ordinary income (see that on page 1 of your return). Schedule D will show the remainder of your losses that you can carry forward to future tax years indefinitely. They can offset an unlimited amount of capital gains in any one year. Know what you have to work with—these losses can be valuable.

Most people just think about what "marginal" tax bracket they are in. Your marginal bracket is the top tier that you fall into when you calculate your tax. So it might be 28% or 35% or something else. Your "effective" tax rate is really more interesting. You calculate it by dividing your total tax owed by your taxable income (both numbers are found on page 2 of your return). This is the true amount of tax that you pay on the income you bring in. It reflects any deductions you might be entitled to and that's why it is almost always lower than your marginal rate.

As you think about your tax rate, you can also consider where you hold your investments—that's called "asset location." The idea is that you should hold certain assets in the types of accounts that give you the greatest advantage. For example, if you are in a high tax bracket, you probably want to minimize investments that throw off taxable income. Instead you want to generate capital gains (that are taxed at lower rates) or tax-exempt interest.

As you review your tax return, consider gains and losses and examine asset location, you'll be in a much better position to answer the question "Is your portfolio tax efficient?" If you find you need to make improvements, make that part of Next Year's Objectives.

Retirement Plan

Projected Retirement Date	*2022*
Current Expenses	*$50,000*
Projected Expenses at Retirement	*$35,000*
On Track?	*Need to run retirement projection to check*

Retirement Considerations

- ✓ Any IRA contributions for current year/any catch-up contributions?
- ✓ Maxing out on company retirement contributions? Match?
- ✓ Any required minimum distributions from retirement accounts?
- ✓ Consider conversion to Roth IRA?
- ✓ Upcoming changes within personal/company retirement plans?
- ✓ Estimated rate of withdrawal: ___%
- ✓ Long-term care insurance? Carrier?

There are usually a whole host of retirement-related decisions surrounding your portfolio. Should you contribute to an IRA? What kind of IRA? Are you putting away as much as you can in your company retirement plan? Any problems with that approach? Are you age 70 ½ and subject to required minimum distributions? If you are taking portfolio withdrawals, do you know the percentage that you are spending? Is it appropriate and sustainable throughout your lifetime? As you think about retirement, have you considered the potentially high costs of medical and nursing home expenses? Do you have a plan to meet those costs? Is long-term care insurance one of your solutions? Are you aware of any problems with your insurance provider?

These questions primarily affect your tax and cash flow planning. You need to allow for enough money to be in cash to meet your needs without jeopardizing the sustainability of your assets over your lifetime.

Education Funding

Child's Name, Age:	Ryan, 10	Emma, 9
Years Until College:	8	9
Type of Funding Vehicle:	529 College Savings Plan	
Balance:	$10,000	$9,000
Contributions:	$1,000 a year for each child	
Date of Last Analysis:	2006	
Change Allocation? (yes/no)	No	
Date of Last Change:	2006	

If you have children, you typically need to think about their investments too. Once they are within four years of starting college, you generally need to start migrating their holdings to more conservative fixed-income investments. While there are many types of college savings accounts, we focus here on 529 Education Savings Plans. For more on other plans, go to www.financial-happiness.com.

If you are concerned about the extreme volatility of the stock market, you may not want to be in the "age-based" types of investment options in 529 Education Savings Plans. These plans put more stock holdings in younger children's portfolios. In theory, that makes sense. But if you're going to get discouraged by major market downturns, you can always create your own asset mix in many 529 plans. Consider a "static mix" where you can choose how much goes into cash accounts, bond funds or stock funds.

Note that 529 Plans only allow changes to investment choices twice a year (as of this date, this rule has not yet been finalized). There are a couple of ways around that you can consider if you are extremely uncomfortable in your current plan. You can transfer the money to another state plan or change the beneficiary of the plan. Both of these options give you the ability to change your investment choices.

Investing for Your Kids

A parent's job is never really done. Paying for a college education is one of the most expensive goals young families have. Some clients want to get a head start on college funding even before the kids are born or in some cases before they are married. I remember one conversation where a very handsome young man was in his first meeting and he had indicated that he wanted to start a college funding account. I could see from his question-naire that he was not married, but we never assume anything, so I asked if there were any children currently. He turned very red and said "no" but that he hoped there would be in the not too distant future. I'm happy to report he did get married in the past year to a beautiful young woman and I think it may be time to fund that college account very soon.

Another client came to us about ten years ago with two girls who were planning to go to college some day. The husband is a police commander and the wife is an executive. We've worked closely on several different major career opportunities for her over the years, but one thing was always constant. They wanted to be sure the girls' money was there when they needed it for college.

Last year the oldest child started attending DePaul University in Chicago. She is a star student and received an impressive financial aid package. Her college debut coincided with the worst stock market since the Great Depression.

Typically we start shifting the investments in college savings accounts to fixed income (cash and bond) starting about four years before the money is actually needed. The experience we just went through with the stock market crash is exactly why we err on the cautious side.

In this case, our client's college money was safely tucked away in cash equivalents, and largely shielded from the bear market. It might not have been earning a lot, but it was there when it was needed. That was peace of mind for the parents and helped them put their money where their hearts are—with their kids.

That bright young woman who started college a year ago interned for our firm this summer. She's a joy to be around and helped our office immeasurably.

Estate Planning:
- ✓ Do you have trust documents?
- ✓ Do you need to update your trust documents?
- ✓ Are your trusts funded?
- ✓ Check beneficiary designations for investment accounts, life insurance policies, retirement plans
- ✓ Gifting strategies?

You want to make sure your investments support the work you've done in planning your estate. If your accounts aren't titled correctly, your plan won't work. So read your estate documents. Check to see that your accounts are titled as your plan dictates. For example, if you have a living trust, you should typically title your taxable account naming yourself as trustee of your trust. You also need to verify your beneficiary designations. Custodians can mistakenly lose these. Or perhaps you didn't fully complete them when you opened the account. Our firm checks once a year to see what's on file at the custodian for each client. If you have a question on who the beneficiary should be, check with the estate attorney who set up your documents.

As you plan your cash flow for the year, you may want to consider gifting. You can give up to $13,000 (in 2009) to as many people as you'd like without having to pay gift tax. You can give an unlimited amount to charity, although your deduction may be limited. You can also give an unlimited amount to your spouse either during life or at death. The question is, can you afford to?

Summary

By completing *The Independent Portfolio Assessment*, you've collected the information you'll need to make intelligent decisions about your investments. As you can see, it's very comprehensive. It touches most areas of your financial life. This approach means that you are integrating your intentions for your money with how you actually execute your decisions. When all of these parts are working in harmony, you stand a much greater chance of attaining satisfaction with your overall approach to financial security.

Client Scorecard

At Stevens Wealth Management, we've created a Client Scorecard that visually reports on what we find as we complete Step One: *The Independent Portfolio Assessment*. This was at the suggestion of a client and created by one of our summer interns. We try to constantly improve our process.

STEVENS
WEALTH MANAGEMENT

Sally and Sam Sample
Personal Scorecard

Current Portfolio Allocation	Target Asset Allocation (IPS)

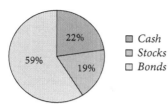

☐ *Cash*
☐ *Stocks*
☐ *Bonds*

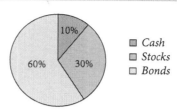

☐ *Cash*
☐ *Stocks*
☐ *Bonds*

Net Worth	Investable Assets

$9,500,000

$2,750,000
Under management (not including outside assets)

Savings Goals	Tax Rates	

☐ *Target 10% of Net*
☑ *Reasonable Debt*

Marginal Federal Rate	35%
Effective Federal Rate	32%
Effective State Rate	3%

Retirement Goals	Insurance Needs

Target Age:

~ *Sally*	70
~ *Sam*	70
Target Investable Assets	$5,500,000
Target Withdrawal Rate	4.60%

☑ *Health*
☐ *Disability*
☑ *Life*
☑ *Home*
☑ *Auto*
☑ *Long-Term Care*

Estate Planning

☑ *Wills*
☑ *Living Trusts*
☑ *Life Insurance Trusts*
☑ *Powers of Attorney*
☑ *Coordinate Beneficiaries*

KEY

☑ *Good*
☐ *Discuss*
■ *Needs Work*

Step Two: The Fundamentals of Finance

I know it's hard to believe we're only on Step Two. But don't you already feel like you know so much more about what you want and where you stand? Next we need to fill in any gaps in your understanding of financial terminology. Step Two of the process is a life-long journey of learning financial concepts—the language of finance. By taking the time to do this, your expectations for investment performance will be more realistic. If you don't understand the basics of the financial world, you'll never really have peace of mind with regard to your portfolio.

Women often ask me if there is a book they could read or a way they can learn more about personal finance. (Men want to know too, but sometimes they don't ask for direction...) To me, the most important concept is balancing risk and reward. We've already touched on that. Implicit in that concept is how to manage risk which may involve diversification or spreading your assets around to many different asset classes. While holding a mix of asset classes can't eliminate risk, it can smooth out the bumps in the road many times.

Asset allocation is a key concept and is again a balancing act. If you can understand these concepts, you'll be well on your way to finding Portfolio Peace of Mind™.

Next you need to understand specific investments. Many of you already own mutual funds or stocks or exchange-traded funds. You need to know what you own. A good resource to help you do this is Morningstar. Their statistical information, especially about expense ratios and actual returns, is very helpful. They also have portfolio tracking tools that can help you quantify your returns.

I've spent the better part of twenty years studying finance and can direct you to some books and resources that have helped me along the way. For good historical background on investing, read Bill Bernstein's books and Jack Bogle's books. Roger Gibson has a classic book on asset allocation. For a modern view of what tomorrow may look like, read *The Post-American World* by Fareed Zakaria. He also has a cable show on CNN (one of the few I think is worth watching). If you want a down-to-earth, easy read I've always enjoyed *The Wealthy Barber* by David Chilton. It's folksy, but practical. Also recommended are Christine Benz's book on mutual funds and Rick Ferri's book on exchange-traded funds. Another good resource is www.bogleheads.org and the related books that Taylor Larimore and Mel Lindauer have coordinated. Never underestimate what you can learn from grassroots advice. Many of these and more are detailed in Appendix C.

In addition, come to the Financial Happiness Library at www.financial-happiness.com to find free information on more topics of interest:

» **Cash and the Current Economic Crisis**
Understanding the risks even in cash.

» **Recognizing Opportunities in a Financial Crisis**
Dealing with what grandma called a "Good Heavens" market.

» **Global Investing**
The U.S. is only a small part of the worldwide investment arena.

» **Demystifying Bonds**
Many people admit they only know very little about
how bonds work.

» **Cleaning Up Gains and Losses**
Learning how to harvest capital gains and losses.

» **Inflation-Linked Bonds in a Deflationary Environment**
Understanding TIPS and I-Bonds.

» **College Funding**
Choosing between 529 Savings Plans and other types of
college savings vehicles.

» **How to Analyze Your Portfolio**
Using an Investment Policy Statement.

» **The Beauty of Asset Location**
Investing for the best tax effect.

» **Tax Considerations for Owners of Company Stock**
Restricted stock, stock options and company stock.
What you need to know.

- » **The World's Poorest Trillionaires**
  Why inflation can seriously derail your investment plans and what to do about it.
- » **Long-Term Care Insurance**
  Weighing the pros and cons.
- » **What to Do If You Lose Your Job**
  A 90-day checklist.
- » **Spending 911**
  Ways to cut expenses.
- » **Give Your 401(k) a Check-Up**
  How to reassess your company retirement plan.
- » **Bear Markets and Retirement**
  How a bear market can impact your retirement plans.
- » **How to Manage Retirement Distributions**
  Navigating penalties and maximizing benefits in retirement
- » **Social Security Tips and Traps**
  Understanding your choices.
- » **Should You Consider a Fixed Annuity**
  Locking in a portion of your retirement income.
- » **A Guide to Caring for Aging Parents**
  Evaluating nursing homes, assisted living or in-home care.
- » **Tips for Reading Your Investment Statements**
  What to look for.
- » **Filing for Bankruptcy**
  Understanding your options.
- » **Dog Bites, Swimming Pools, and Car Crashes**
  Personal property insurance.
- » **Teach Your Kids About Money This Summer**
  Help your kids learn as they work.

Learning about personal finance is ongoing. I'm still learning. That's part of what makes this a fascinating adventure. Don't worry about getting it all down right away. Just jump in, learn to recognize a few new terms and try to remember the basics.

Step Three: Asset Allocation

Deciding how much to invest in stocks versus bonds versus cash is a key element in creating a portfolio that aligns with your ability to take on risk. Jack Bogle, founder of The Vanguard Group, frequently talks about investing your age in bonds. So at age 80, he has about 80% of his portfolio in bonds. At a recent conference, as part of a panel of experts including Bill Bernstein and Rick Ferri (both well-respected financial advisors and authors), we were asked whether we agreed with this statement.

Overall, it makes sense. Of course, there can be exceptions. If you are investing for future generations, then you're investing beyond your life expectancy. Or if you have a windfall at a young age, then you may want to be more conservative in order to preserve your wealth.

If you hire professional investment management, you can expect that your advisor will get much more sophisticated about not only broader asset allocation, but sub-allocation. That's how to divide money up between different types of stocks or bonds for greater diversification benefits.

You can do that as an individual investor too. Two classic books that have good discussions on asset allocation are Roger Gibson's *Asset Allocation* and Bill Bernstein's *The Four Pillars of Investing*. After the melt-down in 2008-2009, some people question the value of asset allocation and the concept of diversification. After all, in this period, just about everything went down. But having been in the thick of this mess steering the ship, I know that portfolios that were allocated to an appropriate mix of stocks and bonds suffered far less than portfolios that held higher percentages of stock. Diversification doesn't mean you won't suffer losses, it just means that you spread the risk around. It helps manage risk, but it can't eliminate it.

At Stevens Wealth Management, we practice "tactical asset allocation" as well as "strategic asset allocation." "Strategic" allocation is setting the broad parameters of the portfolio. It covers how much you want to hold in cash, bonds and stocks. "Tactical" allocation builds some flexibility into the allocation so that you can adjust up or down on the percentage in each sub-asset class depending on many factors including market conditions, economic issues and so forth. Some people contend that this constitutes "market timing." And in some sense they are correct. However, we use our tactical allocations sparingly and have found it improves our returns and generally provides greater consistency. When we set asset class ranges in our IPS's, we think about how low we would go in a market crash and how high we would go if the market soars as it relates to each client's objectives and risk tolerance.

In the past I've written articles using model portfolios for conservative, moderate and aggressive investors. I'm not going to do that here, although you can find examples in some of the books I'm recommending in Appendix C. At Stevens Wealth Management, we create customized portfolios for each client. Typically, new clients come in the door with all kinds of existing investments. Many times there are significant tax implications of selling. We take all of that into account as we design a proposed portfolio. Sometimes it can take quite a while to implement our recommendations as we manage the tax and other constraints.

We tend to use more "passive" investments than "active." "Passive" investments are index funds that replicate certain segments of the market. "Active" implies the manager of a mutual fund is trying to beat the market. You can find good passive investments at The Vanguard Group that offer low costs. We also use Dimensional Fund Advisors (DFA Funds) that are only available through approved advisors as well as many other types of assets.

Although we generally advocate passive investing, many of our clients still choose to hold individual stocks for a portion of their portfolio. There's nothing wrong with this and in fact it can inspire people who are choosing those investments to follow their hearts. The key is balance and proportion and following the same key principles of risk and reward we've outlined above. Just remember, if your goal is Portfolio Peace of Mind™, it can be achieved with a passive approach and an appropriate asset allocation.

Jason Zweig, columnist at *The Wall Street Journal*, has written a good book about behavioral finance called *Your Money & Your Brain*. Behavioral finance is the study of how our emotions affect investment decisions. One of the concepts covered is over-confidence. I've seen this happen repeatedly and I have to constantly keep this in check myself.

Let me tell you a story about over-confidence and asset allocation. I remember talking to a client several months before the market started going south about his asset allocation. We managed a portion of his money and he managed the rest himself. If you use the "invest your age in bonds" allocation rule of thumb, he was far too aggressive. But it had paid big returns for twenty years until he came to 2000. He was over-confident and overly aggressive. This could have been a recipe for disaster. Fortunately, I convinced him that we should start moving both portions of his portfolio to a more appropriate, conservative mix of assets. Good thing. Within months the stock market shed 55%, but because he overcame this common behavioral pitfall, we managed to preserve a much greater portion of his net worth.

Step Four: Investment Policy Statements

Think of your Investment Policy Statement as your personal set of instructions that allows you to fly your investment plane even in very turbulent conditions. It's what would help Sully land his plane in the Hudson River if he was navigating a portfolio.

An Investment Policy Statement is your key to investment success. You create it by thinking through a number of situations before they happen and commit your intentions to writing. When times get tough, you stick to your IPS. It creates a discipline and helps you avoid mistakes driven by emotion.

> » Investment policies should communicate a clear statement of objectives
> » Cash flow requirements should be considered in setting the investment policy
> » Policies and guidelines are driven by risk tolerance, size of the portfolio and investment choices
> » Disciplined control procedures for evaluating portfolio performance, assessing progress toward objectives and rebalancing should be outlined and implemented

Sample IPS Criteria

Portfolio Objectives	Growth, income, stability of principal, range of expected returns based on forward- and backward-looking statistics	Comfortable retirement, college funding
Cash Flow Requirements	Required minimum distributions, calculated withdrawal rates	Per objective
Current Assets	Current balance	Per objective
Time Horizon	Number of years until money is needed	Period over which money will be distributed
Managing Risk	Longevity risk: is there time to re-accumulate assets? Depth of diversification	Loss aversion Propensity to panic Loss limits? Dollar cost average?
Expected Return	Target percent over inflation	Based on averages for asset allocation mixes
Portfolio Structure	Specific percentages +/- 5% per sub-asset class	Focus often on broad asset classes and time horizon
Selection Criteria	Mutual funds or managers must adhere to objective	Low expenses Track record Rank among peers
Control Procedures	Quarterly performance reports Frequency of reviews	Re-examine Investment Policy Statement annually; Rebalance

The headings on the left side of the chart should make up the sections of your IPS. You can keep this simple and just create a document that comments on your expectations for each of these areas. In the past, we've had IPS statements that were twelve-to-fifteen pages long at Stevens Wealth Management. Now we've boiled that down to two pages. It doesn't need to be elaborate. It just needs to highlight key areas of your investment plan.

As you complete your own Investment Policy Statement, you will need current statistics for expected investment returns. These change based on historical data and also on forward-looking projections of what people think is reasonable to expect in the future. For thoughts on what these numbers should be, take a look at The Bogle eBlog at http://johncbogle.com. You'll find Jack's latest speeches that frequently comment on this type of data. You may also find reasonable expectations at www.bogleheads.org.

By thinking through how you will handle your investments in a variety of economic scenarios, you set clear direction and parameters for portfolio monitoring and rebalancing. During times of extreme market volatility, a carefully constructed IPS can help prevent panic and help you stay the course. I've had many people come up to me over the years and tell me how this document really did change their whole approach to investing.

Update your IPS annually using current market statistics to see what returns are reasonable given your mix of assets. This also gives you a chance to see if you want to adjust any of the ranges for your asset class targets.

Steps Five and Six: Implementing, Rebalancing and Monitoring Your Portfolio

Let's review: You've analyzed your investing situation thoroughly. You understand the basics of combining risk and reward. You've set your mix of stocks and bonds and outlined your expectations for the portfolio in an IPS. Now it's time to take action and rebalance your portfolio.

In the implementation phase, you'll rebalance your current holdings to match the broad asset allocation guidelines you've set in your IPS. You should also examine each holding to see if it is consistent with your expectations of low fees, low anxiety and congruence with your personal beliefs. Morningstar.com is a good source to help you do much of this. Compare your holdings to the category average as you think about its place in your portfolio.

Your job isn't done once you've made changes to your portfolio. You'll need to keep an eye on it. At a minimum, look at your investments once a month. You can do this when you get your statement from your custodian or you can go online. Sites like www.vanguard.com or www.morningstar.com will let you enter your entire portfolio and monitor the results.

Once a quarter, look at the overall asset allocation and compare it to your IPS asset class parameters. See if you are within plus or minus 5% of those ranges. Most of the time you will not need to rebalance, but if there have been extreme market conditions, you may need to. When you assess your progress in the context of what's realistic, you will get a better feel for the natural ebb and flow of the markets and you'll gain confidence in the overall process.

Here are a few guidelines to help you in the rebalancing and monitoring processes:

» As you review your brokerage statement each month, check the beginning and ending balance to see how your assets have changed. Review any additions or withdrawals from the accounts. Review transactions and brokerage fees for accuracy.

» If you receive quarterly performance reports from an investment advisor, look at the percentage and dollar change in your assets. Compare your returns to appropriate benchmarks. Make sure your cost basis has been accurately recorded. If you don't know how to read your reports, ask your advisor to send you something that walks you through each line. Most of us have something like that to help you. Or have a conversation with your advisor to help explain the report.

» Annually, review your objectives. What progress have you made in the last year? What challenges and opportunities arose? How should you address those going forward?

» Once a year complete a new *Independent Portfolio Assessment* to see what you need to do next.

» Celebrate when you meet your goals. Re-group if you find you are coming up short and need to increase your savings or change your strategic approach.

At Stevens Wealth Management, we do all of the above in addition to following a thorough process that analyzes how each specific investment is doing relative to its peers, screens investments by category for new ideas that meet our criteria (although that doesn't necessarily mean we make a change), gauges how economic factors could affect our investment choices, periodically re-examine our broad asset class ranges for potential adjustments and so forth.

One of the articles that I used to write annually for Morningstar was an overview of Jack Bogle's portfolio. Over time, one of the many things I learned from Jack was "if it ain't broke, don't fix it." If his asset allocation was consistent with his objectives, he didn't make any changes. Sometimes for years at a time. He kept his costs low—of course! He allocated a certain amount to charity. And he focused on index funds. I've carried those lessons over into the way I manage money for myself and my clients today.

The six-step Comprehensive Investment Process forms a circle. Each year as you review your portfolio you'll follow the same six steps. The first time is the hardest because many of these issues will be new to you and require some thought. In future years, the process will usually flow more easily.

The discipline of a sound process will give you something to hang on to when times get tough. And we've seen plenty of that in recent years. Critical thinking is especially valuable when all around you is uncertainty and fear. Holding fast to principles that have passed the test of time will help you steer a clear course to peace of mind.

> *Even the most brilliant of mathematical geniuses*
> *will never be able to tell us what the future holds.*
> *In the end, what matters is the quality*
> *of our decisions in the face of uncertainty.*
>
> ~ Peter Bernstein

Aligning Your Values

This chapter is about Portfolio Peace of Mind™. We've covered how balancing risk and reward help you toward this goal. And you've just seen how a disciplined process can help you make sound financial decisions even in the face of extreme adversity. But the final element is making sure that when you invest, you feel good about what you are doing.

I started the Introduction with a story about a socially conscious investor whose portfolio was not aligned with his values. He knew something wasn't right, but until we dug into his specific holdings, he didn't know where his money was going. To be fully congruent in how you live your life, it helps to invest in things you believe in and that you think can benefit people around the world.

There are several ways to approach this. First, you can choose to invest through a sound process and use the profits to fund your goals for yourself and those you love. That puts your money where your heart is. Alternatively, you can implement your investment decisions using a layer of socially conscious investments. There are plenty to choose from and they are increasing constantly. But it's not as straight-forward as you might hope.

My advice is to follow the six-step process above and add in an additional layer that emphasizes social consciousness. You can add something to your Investment Policy Statement (Step Four) that states that your preference is for investments that promote sustainability or environmental protection or whatever you care about. In Step Five, where you implement your changes and rebalance, you can screen investments that fit your asset class preferences and see if there are any good socially conscious alternatives that fit in your desired asset mix. For example, you may choose a socially conscious mutual fund to fill part of your large-cap stock allocation.

Increased Interest in a Social Agenda

In the past two years, assets in socially responsible investments in the U.S. have surged 18% (versus 3% for managed assets in general). That's $2.71 trillion being invested in socially conscious securities. Clearly investors are increasingly aligning their financial intentions with their social activism.

President Obama is one of those socially conscious investors. According to reports from 2008, he invested about half of his portfolio in the Vanguard FTSE Social Index Fund (VFTSX). Not only is he investing his own money in socially responsible investments (SRI), but his social agenda for the country includes putting people to work on projects improving our infrastructure and environment. Whether you agree with the President's politics or not, you may choose to put your money into the projects and causes that are most important to you.

But investing in socially conscious funds or stocks or exchange-traded funds is not as simple as it may appear. It is loaded with contradictions and paradoxes. For example, look at one of the largest socially conscious mutual funds available–the Vanguard FTSE Social Index Fund (VFTSX). While the expense ratio is very low, as it is for most Vanguard funds, performance has lagged the category over the past several years. A quick look at the underlying securities, as reported by Morningstar, show a number of big banks in the top holdings. In thinking about what happened in the recent past in the financial services area, there may be widely varying opinions on whether these firms really have socially conscious intentions at their core.

Socially responsible mutual funds have been around for nearly two decades, and as a group, their track record has been, well, mediocre. But that may be changing. As with anything, the more attention an area gets, the more talent is drawn to it. As we look at these types of investments going forward, we want to pay particular attention to expense ratios and how the funds compare with their not necessarily socially responsible peer groups. While some investors are willing to forgo the most profitable returns, these vehicles should be at least competitive.

Aligning your values with how you choose to invest your money brings more meaning to the process. You are more likely to be engaged because more than just your head is involved. It feels good to be a part of the solution and to make money. *Put Your Money Where Your Heart Is* is not about blindly making wild investments without thought. It's about carefully constructing a portfolio that is well-researched, balanced, personally satisfying and that can meet reasonable expectations.

Let me share a brief story that sums up Portfolio Peace of Mind™ and Putting Your Money Where Your Heart Is:

Bird Watching Mandatory

A good friend of mine called me shortly after the worst of the financial meltdown and asked me if I would meet with a close friend of hers that was devastated after having lost a considerable portion of her retirement nest egg. She just didn't know how she would recover and was having a tough time functioning. She represented millions of others in similar circumstances.

Of course I agreed to meet with her. At our first meeting, it was clear that this woman was in shock. Although she had expressed her discomfort with the risk and loss levels in her portfolio to her prior advisor, no action was taken to change her portfolio throughout the financial crisis. She finally pulled her money, but at the bottom of the market crash (at least so far—who knows what may happen in the future).

So the question at hand was how to proceed. She distrusted the stock market and did not want to take the same kind of risk that she had in the past. She also needed to sell her home in order to raise more capital to live on. The house has been on the market for several months now with no activity.

We repositioned her portfolio so it is now aligned with her values and her risk tolerance. Does that mean it won't ever go down again? Of course not. But hopefully the losses will be more manageable because her portfolio is better aligned with her risk tolerance. We've found ways to create greater security going forward.

We spent a considerable amount of time talking about spending. This was the key to finding a reasonable course of action going forward. Once she understood this was the way to pull herself out of this "hole," she attacked her spending needs with great enthusiasm. She figured out how much she would need while she was still in her house and how much she would need after that. We ran a retirement projection that included modeling how a fixed immediate annuity could provide a guaranteed income stream for the rest of her life.

And we also included an annual spending amount for bird watching, her beloved pastime. I think that's when she started to feel better. I could see her light up when she saw it in her budget. No matter how much money she had—or didn't have—she would be able to follow her heart. No matter how tough things get, it's important to use your money for the things you really love in life. That's putting your money where your heart is. And only time will tell, but we hope this repositioning of her portfolio combined with a disciplined process will bring her peace of mind.

Summary

I warned you at the beginning of this chapter that investing is an expansive topic. We've covered three important areas: Balancing Risk and Reward, Creating a Six-Step Comprehensive Investment Process and Aligning Your Values with how you allocate your assets. You now have tools you can use to examine how your investments integrate with every other area of personal finance. You can create balance in your portfolio and increase your chances of success by designing a meaningful Investment Policy Statement.

Next we'll tackle It's Not Just Retirement, It's the Rest of Your Life™. Another very expansive topic. Retirement is no longer a gold watch and a few more years of life. Retirement is the next great adventure and people are choosing to make major life changes at all ages.

A Necessary Autumn Inside Each

You and I have spoken all these words, but as for the way
We have to go, words

Are no preparation. There is no getting ready, other than
Grace. My faults

Have stayed hidden. One might call that a preparation!
I have one small drop

Of knowing in my soul. Let it dissolve in your ocean.
There are so many threats to it.

Inside each of us, there's continual autumn. Our leaves
Fall and are blown out

Over the water. A crow sits in the blackened limbs and talks
About what's gone. Then

Your generosity returns: spring, moisture, intelligence, the
Scent of hyacinth and rose

And cypress. And if you don't feel in
Yourself the freshness of

Joseph, be Jacob! Weep and then smile. Don't pretend to know
Something you haven't experienced.

There's a necessary dying, and then Jesus is breathing again.
Very little grows on jagged

Rock. Be ground. Be crumbled, so wildflowers will come up
Where you are. You've been

Stony for too many years. Try something different. Surrender.

~ Jelaluddin Rumi

Chapter 5

It's Not Just Retirement, It's the Rest of Your Life™

Take a Chance, Start Over, Reset your Compass

The "necessary autumn" that Rumi speaks of is at the heart of this next chapter. In this context, you can re-create yourself at any point in time. So you see, a new beginning is not just retirement, it's the rest of your life.

> "Whatever you can do, or dream you can, begin it.
> Boldness has genius, power and magic in it."
> ~ Goethe

Dare to Dream

Making big changes in your life is both scary and exciting. I know. I've taken that quantum leap on more than one occasion.

Life should be an adventure. Some of you may be perfectly content doing what you're doing and that's just fine. Some of you may not have thought about other challenges you'd like to take in life in quite a while. But perhaps you'd like to give this some consideration. Some of you may not have a choice—I've seen many situations over the years where a job loss or a health problem meant a major change often unexpectedly.

No matter where you are in life, making a major decision to change takes courage and forethought. Here's my Major Life Transition Checklist to get you started thinking through your choices:

Major Life Transition Checklist

✔ *Where are you going to live?*

As you face major changes, where you choose to live is usually involved. If you are retiring, you may be thinking about moving to a warmer climate. Or perhaps splitting your time between two locations. If you are taking a new job, it may involve relocation. If you want to make a career change, you may need to downsize where you live. Or at some point you may be considering some type of continuing care community that requires a move.

✔ *What are you going to do?*

If you are making a change for career reasons, this will probably be obvious. If you are retiring, it may take some thought. Most people want to have an idea of what their lives will be like before they take the plunge to make major changes. Most retirees I talk to are plenty busy. They volunteer, spend time with family, golf, garden—whatever draws them closer to their hearts.

✔ *What will that cost?*

Your vision of the future has a price tag. You need to have a pretty good idea of what that is before you transition. As you work through your current budget, list what will change. Investigate what those new activities will cost. The closer you can get to reality, the better prepared you will be.

✔ *Have you accumulated enough money to take that chance?*

This may be the million dollar question—literally. If you are retiring, you need to know that the money you've accumulated will last as long as you do. Even if you are contemplating a major job change, you may need to rely on accumulated assets for a short period while you re-establish yourself in your new field. You will probably need to run a cash flow projection to be able to answer this question thoroughly.

✔ *How will you stay connected?*

In Chapter One, we talked about staying connected as one of the paths to financial (or just plain old) happiness. The decisions you make affect other people too. You need to think through how you will keep your connections to people, places and things you love. That will help give you support and stability as you launch new efforts.

✔ *Have you thought through health care decisions?*

Your health is always a priority. Many people are fortunate to have health insurance when they are working. If you make a major life transition, you need to think about how you will pay for health care. That may be new company coverage, private health insurance (new legislation has not been passed as I write this), Medicare or perhaps long-term care at some point.

Stories of Change

Before we jump into analysis and number crunching, let's see how some people have changed their lives by carefully weighing the financial pros and cons. Making major life changes shouldn't be something anyone does quickly or without serious thought, but it can open the door to a whole new beginning.

Taking a Chance on a New Business

Often the scariest times in life are when we try something new. Over the years I've helped many clients make the transition from the "big corporate job" to something more entrepreneurial. It's never an easy decision and it's not for everyone, but it can be well worth the risk.

Denis is a client who worked for a major philanthropic foundation. He had a very successful career, but wanted to try something on his own.

Here's his story:

> *"Having never run my own business, I was terrified at the financial ramifications of that decision and what would happen were the business to fail. With Sue's guidance, I developed a business plan, including contingencies for a slow start-up and potential failure. Fortunately, the failure scenarios we developed never came to pass; still, without Sue's support and assurance, I would not have had the confidence to jump ship and the sense of security that comes from knowing how all the 'what-ifs' could be handled."*

He literally Put His Money Where His Heart Was. We started by developing "what-if" scenarios. To do this it's helpful to use some type of cash flow modeling software. That's what we do at Stevens Wealth Management. I've seen many do-it-yourself versions of Excel spreadsheets that cover many of the critical factors, but they often omit important considerations like taxes or inflation or required minimum distributions from retirement accounts. This is one area where it really can help to hire a professional.

Happily, Denis's consulting business has been a wild success. He is much in demand and has been able to make many wonderful changes to his life. He is happily married and owns a sprawling ranch outside of Bozeman, Montana. I've been fortunate enough to visit he and his wife there and loved seeing nature unspoiled. They are able to enjoy life, hike in the mountains, ski in the winter and travel the country in their cute little RV powered by a Mercedes-Benz diesel engine.

Putting your money where your heart is requires courage. And sometimes despite exceptional planning, things don't turn out the way you'd hoped. But knowing that you "went for it" makes life worth living. And it's the journey that's worth taking regardless of the final destination. Happily, in Denis's case, it worked out beautifully.

Time in Tahiti

Years ago I was speaking at a money conference in L.A. when I met Shelly. She heard me speak and sought me out. Her husband had died from cancer five years earlier and she was trying to figure out what to do next. Her heart was broken, but she knew she needed to create a life for herself and her son that allowed them to find peace and re-discover happiness.

She decided to move to Tahiti and raise her seven-year old son. Shelly was well-traveled, so she knew she could handle cultural change:

> *"On my first trip to Moorea, French Polynesia, my mouth just dropped as I was struck by the natural beauty of the tropical vegetation and colors of the beach and lagoon; I fell in love with it immediately upon arrival and the Tahitians were exceptional too. I went home to L.A., but became 'home-sick' for Moorea. I flew back, two weeks later, with my only son at 7 years old–he liked it too. On my third trip, two months later, I made my decision to live there. And seven months later, I made that happen."*

Warning: Homework Required

If you are contemplating moving abroad, you need to do some legwork ahead of time. Shelly visited the area and read up on customs and culture. One book she recommends is *The Grown-Up's Guide to Running Away from Home* by Rosanne Knorr, which contained a quiz that asked some important questions including:

» Are you interested in learning more about other cultures?
» Are you willing to learn a new language?
» Are you adaptable when it comes to finding new interests and activities?
» Are you able to handle stress?
» Are you in good health?
» Do you have a sense of adventure?

> *"I said yes to all of the questions...I was on my way. I was ready to prepare myself mentally and physically for this adventure."*

Shelly's advice for you?

> *"Talk to as many people as possible who have already had the experience. Make sure it's the right country for you, explore as much as possible–you'll know once you are there."*

Expect a Few Bumps in the Road or Snakes in the Pool
Nothing is ever easy, is it? The best thing we can do is stay flexible and roll with the punches. For example, when I moved to Pennsylvania to work for The Vanguard Group, I chose to live in the beautiful rolling hills out in the country. It offered spectacular scenery, fresh air, and even a historic 200-year-old barn. I didn't know about the occasional snakes in the pool, that wells and septic systems are expensive to repair, and that bats in the barn can surprise you. I wouldn't trade the experience for anything, but there were a few hitches.

Shelly offers this advice: *"Watch the languages if you must learn a new one. Sometimes your lack of understanding the words can mean you are taken advantage of. The hardest thing for me was getting over my intimidation when speaking French. I knew 'oui' and 'no,' but that's about it."*

Although Shelly has recently moved back to California as her son is now nearly grown, she says *"The best experiences are waking up every day with a new adventure–whether it's small or not. As a widow, the thing I have realized is that life is short. So I strive to live for every day. I have gained more in my experiences of life from having an open mind. I love culture and people. It's always a new experience."*

Before you make any major life decisions, do your homework. Here are a few guidelines for this situation:

> » Check out the cost of living in your target retirement location. Compare renting with buying. Think about how much your expenses would be and then add a cushion for unexpected costs.

> » Evaluate any income potential you have in the new location. Can your portfolio provide some cash flow? Can you collect Social Security?

> » Make sure you understand how you will be taxed and how that may affect retirement income.

> » Medicare will not cover you if you live in a foreign country (with some limited exceptions). So think about how you will pay for health care costs.

Working a Little Longer
Many of our clients are just about to retire or are in the early years of retirement. This is a particularly nerve-wracking place to be in life given what we've just experienced with the financial markets. Gail planned to retire in

early 2009 in her mid 50s. We'd done our planning and up until recently it looked like a "go." Her husband has already retired and financially they are well off.

But Gail watched her 401(k) plan take a big hit. We discussed the investment choices and asset allocation several times, but short of shifting to all Stable Value (which had its own issues with liquidity), losses were unavoidable. There was no money market choice in the plan (just the Stable Value fund) and the one bond choice was expensive and not particularly well-rated (although we did use it because we needed a fixed-income holding). Even the balanced fund was down over -20%.

So we decided to run a new retirement projection for Gail and her husband. This time the probability of success was lower than any of us wanted. So we discussed the options, which included working part-time for a few more years. Gail likes the work she does, so although it wasn't her first choice, she decided that having the financial security of an income for a few more years was worth it. She is also relatively young to be retiring and that entered into the decision too.

Company Stock Meltdown

Many of you may have heard the warnings from most financial advisors about holding too much in company stock. It's risky not only because you are concentrating so much of your nest egg's growth on just one company, but also because a plunging stock price combined with layoffs could double the financial hit. But sometimes paring back the one stock you know most closely is hard to do. Part of that can be emotional and part can be based on a strong belief in the company's future.

Jack experienced a 50%+ drop in his company stock in 2008. And he saw his net worth drop almost in half too. He had a heavy concentration in company stock when he came in to work with us and his portfolio was over 90% in the stock market. He and his wife had just retired and now they were worried he might have to go back to work.

We immediately worked to reposition his portfolio to a more appropriate mix of stocks, bonds and cash. We also found ways to net out gains and losses with part of his company stock so that he could diversify more and not incur a lot of taxes by selling large quantities of stock. He and his wife are now in a much better position to recover from this financial setback and enjoy these active years of their retirement.

Jack and his wife have plenty of money to retire comfortably. He is able to put his money where his heart is for his family, philanthropically, and through his ongoing business leadership.

Sale of a Business

We have several clients who have recently sold a business and are now transitioning to a new part of their lives. In some cases, they are still working and in some cases they are shifting to a new life in retirement.

Bob and Christine are in their 70s and are transitioning from suburbia to a brand new continuing care retirement community. They are excited and optimistic about the future. He retired a few years ago and she just sold her business. Their niece called us a few months ago because she was very worried about their current investments (managed by another advisor). They were losing money fast and their mix of stocks and bonds was out of whack.

In repositioning their portfolio, we needed to keep their income needs in mind. They not only required the balance due for their new retirement community, but they needed their portfolio to generate enough income (along with their pensions and Social Security) to pay their new monthly assessments and expenses. Using cash from the recent sale of a home as well as her business, we were able to carve out assets for their new living arrangement and design a portfolio that generates sufficient income to meet their needs. We also repositioned their existing assets to reduce the risk they were taking and lower overall costs.

Cash Flow Planning

What all these stories have in common is that we had to spend a good deal of time thinking about cash flow and contingency planning before they actually made life changes. Given the significant impact the stock market has had on assets since the fall of 2007, anyone planning a major life transition needs to re-evaluate what the decrease in assets means to their planning and how that translates to saving and spending.

The people most vulnerable to these past events are those close to or in retirement. Common sense tells you that if you have significantly less assets, you may have to adjust your spending levels. And yet many people are in denial about that. The consequences of not addressing this issue could be catastrophic. Many times the greatest fear we see is that of running out of money and becoming a burden to loved ones.

If you take a step back and look at this situation from a higher elevation, higher levels of savings are really the only reasonable solution. Just about everyone in the U.S. is going to need to save more. That means spending less. And that will slow the economic recovery because so much of this country's GDP (gross domestic product) is dependent on consumer spending. But saving more (and spending less) is the only lasting solution to this problem of asset depletion.

We've seen the pendulum of unwise use of credit swing too far in the past several decades. Many people have lost touch with what it means to overextend themselves on credit cards or mortgages. Part of what we are experiencing is a rebalancing of that system.

So how do you know how much you can spend? If you are working, you can keep it simple and save a percentage of your income. If you've lost ground in the past ten years in the stock market, that probably means you need to save 10-20% of your take-home pay after contributing as much as possible to a retirement plan. If you are already retired, you need to think about "withdrawal rates."

How Much Can You Spend in Retirement?

The subject of withdrawal rates is complex and at times nerve-wracking. Almost everyone worries about running out of money some day. Finding the appropriate spending level is key to solving that problem. It's really a matter of finding the right balance between what you've accumulated and what you need as you draw down your assets in retirement.

There are many factors that affect how much you can spend: your mix of stocks and bonds in your portfolio, tax rates, inflation, Social Security, pensions, required minimum distributions from retirement accounts to name some. There have been many studies done about withdrawal rates, but most of them fail to consider all of these factors.

We've devised a simple tool you can use to get an approximation of what you can spend in retirement. For those of you with complicated situations, it is critical to get customized professional help.

A Simple Guide to Retirement Spending

Part I: Determine Your Withdrawal Rate

Step 1: Find the closest number of years you expect to live in retirement
Step 2: Find the closest target asset mix to your own
Step 3: Find the intersection of those two columns to find your 1st year target withdrawal rate

Step 1: Years Expected in Retirement	Step 2: Asset Mix		
	Conservative ~ 33% Cash ~ 33% Taxable Bonds ~ 34% Stocks	Moderate ~ 10% Cash ~ 50% Taxable Bonds ~ 40% Stocks	Aggressive ~ 10% Cash ~ 30% Taxable Bonds ~ 60% Stocks
15	5.86%	6.00%	5.93%
25	3.43%	3.60%	3.60%
35	2.37%	2.52%	2.53%

Assumptions:

~ *Cash rate of return is 2%*
~ *Taxable bond rate of return is 4.5%*
~ *Stock rate of return is 7%*
~ *$500,000 portfolio: 50% in taxable assets, 50% in retirement accounts*
~ *RMDs start at age 70 1/2*
~ *Includes tax at current rates on retirement distributions and portfolio income*
~ *90% probability of success*
~ *Standard deviation in probability analysis increases with risk in asset mix*
~ *Inflation is 3.5% with a range of -1% (deflation) to 7% in probability analysis*

Part II: How Much Can You Spend in Retirement?

Step 1: Total your taxable investable assets *Add together your brokerage accounts, mutual funds, stocks, bonds and other taxable assets*	*A*
Step 2: Total your retirement assets *Add together your IRAs, 401ks, 403(b)s, 457s and other retirement assets*	*B*
Step 3: Find your effective tax rate (federal and state) *Divide total tax paid by total taxable income.* *Add federal and state rates together.*	*C*
Step 4: Calculate the after-tax value of retirement assets *Multiply your retirement assets (B) by (1 minus C)*	*D*
Step 5: Sum your after-tax assets (A + D)	*E*
Step 6: Apply your withdrawal rate to your after-tax assets (X% times E) *Find your withdrawal rate in Part I and multiply times E in Part II*	*F*
Step 7: Total your after-tax income from other sources *Sum your Social Security, pension and other income sources after-tax* *To find the after-tax amount, multiple the pre-tax amount by (1 minus C)*	*G*
Step 8: Determine your retirement spending total	*F + G*

This simple worksheet we've developed assumes you spend your money during your lifetime. If you want to leave money to family or charities, subtract that amount from your after-tax assets (E). This approach does not factor in estate taxes after you die. Again, for more complex planning, work with a professional.

Asset Mix

Given that stock returns have been so paltry over the past ten years, more people are choosing to hold a lower stock allocation in their portfolios. Will that approach turn out to be more advantageous? No one knows. But you can't ignore the effect it will have on your retirement planning.

There is a point of diminishing returns when you add more stocks to your mix in these analyses. More stocks do not always translate to more spending power. The volatility of stocks can actually decrease the withdrawal rate at a certain point.

Tilting more toward the bond side of the portfolio does not guarantee success either. Inflation and other factors erode the purchasing power of the portfolio. You really need a balanced mix of stocks and bonds.

In Part I, Step 1, choose the mix of assets that is closest to your target retirement portfolio. If you change the mix in your portfolio over time, you'll need to revisit your withdrawal rate.

Longevity

The number of years your money needs to last also has a dramatic effect on your withdrawal rate. Most of the studies that are quoted show about a 4% rate—but that usually applies to a 25 year life expectancy. Those studies usually are looking at a 65 year-old who lives to age 90.

But what if you live past age 90? Unless you've set up a fixed annuity with inflation protection, you could run out of money or lose purchasing power. (This is not to imply that you should put all of your money in immediate annuities. They have pros and cons too.)

If you expect to live longer than 25 years, your withdrawal rate will be lower (and vice versa).

In Part I, Step 2, you choose the number of years that is closest to what you think you will have in retirement. Remember people are living longer. Most planning models assume a life expectancy into the 90s to be conservative.

Probability

After the extreme market losses we've seen in recent years, there has been criticism of many of the probability models used in retirement planning. These models vary the levels of returns and inflation in hundreds or thousands of simulations, but if the standard deviation of those factors is not set high enough, it may underestimate the highs and lows that the models show. (No one is really worried about the highs.)

At this point, there is nothing I've found that is better than these models (assuming the advisor uses appropriate standard deviations and realistic return data) to factor in cash flows, tax effects, required minimum distributions and so forth. In this Simple Retirement Spending Worksheet, we have chosen an acceptable probability percentage of 90%. That means 90% of the time withdrawals do not deplete the assets throughout the retirement period. It also means the rate of withdrawal is lower than it would be if we decreased the acceptable probability to 75% or 80%.

Key to this analysis is revising the assumptions and calculations every year or so. That gives you a chance to revisit the spending levels and adjust as necessary.

Withdrawal Rate

Using the chart on page 86, find the withdrawal rate that corresponds to asset mix and years in retirement. This percentage can be applied to your after-tax asset value to determine how much you can withdraw from your portfolio in the initial year of retirement. That can be added to the after-tax total income you have from other sources like Social Security, pensions or fixed annuities.

If you take dividends and interest from your portfolio, that counts as part of your withdrawal rate.

If you aren't happy with how much you can spend, you probably need to accumulate more. That's easier said than done depending on where you are in life. You may need to think creatively about sharing living space with someone (family, a roommate). Or you may need to really scrub those expense numbers. Whatever method you choose, the bottom line is that you may need to find a way to live on less.

Our model assumes a portfolio with 50% in retirement assets that will be taxed in the future and 50% in assets already taxed (future growth being taxed at capital gains rates as assets are sold). We build in required minimum distributions on the retirement assets. We've factored in 3.5% inflation every year, but our probability model varies that over time. Asset class returns are conservative (cash is 2%, taxable bonds are 4.5% and stocks are 7%). These are nominal returns (before inflation). If we have more stocks in the portfolio, the volatility (standard deviation) of the returns is higher.

Expert Opinions

You'll see many experts predict that you can use higher withdrawal rates in retirement. And they may be right. It all depends on the assumptions used in the analysis. Results vary depending on whether you factor in taxable and retirement accounts, required minimum distributions, asset mixes with less than 50% in stocks, higher inflation rates and so forth.

One of the best books I've read on this subject is Bill Bengen's *Conserving Client Portfolios During Retirement*. It's meant for advisors, but many of you will find it fascinating. You can also find good information at Bill's website www.billbengen.com. Bill is a financial advisor in California. In addition, both Jonathan Guyton, Principal of Cornerstone Wealth Advisors, and Michael Kitces, Director of Financial Planning for Pinnacle Advisory Group, are doing excellent research on this important topic of withdrawal rates.

Retirement Projections

A simple worksheet may be fine for getting a sense of what you can spend in retirement, but for major decision-making you should probably work with an advisor who can use sophisticated retirement modeling software. As you can tell from the stories I've shared, we use this approach extensively at Stevens Wealth Management. There are some online calculators that are accessible to everyone, but you must be extremely cautious about the underlying assumptions.

Fixed Immediate Annuities:
A Guaranteed Income Stream for Life

As you think about sources of income in retirement, you may want to consider locking in a minimum level of spending. When I first started counseling retirees, many of them had pension plans. That gave them a fixed stream of income, not much different from when they received a paycheck while working. But now pension plans are much less common. If you want a guaranteed retirement income, you may have to do-it-yourself.

What's a Fixed Immediate Annuity?

Basically it's a series of payments that start immediately. It can be "qualified" which means it's funded with retirement dollars and is taxed when the payments are made. Or it can be "non-qualified" which means you use after-tax money to set it up, and distributions are free from federal tax.

It's invested in "fixed income." That's usually bonds and cash equivalents. An insurance company underwrites the annuity and they promise to pay you for life. So make sure the insurance company is on solid financial footing. You need them to be around for at least your lifetime to make good on their promise. You can check life insurance ratings by purchasing the annual ratings issue of *The Insurance Forum* at www.theinsuranceforum. com/pages/ratings.html.

When you purchase the annuity, it has a set interest rate that you'll receive. That's "fixed." This type of annuity is not deferred to start paying out at some future date. So it's "immediate."

Watch out for the costs on any annuity. They are issued by insurance companies and the costs can vary widely. I like low costs on all types of investments, but you really have to pay attention with annuities. It's not uncommon to find a lot of bells and whistles on annuity products that can get really costly. There are fees for the underlying investments (similar to mutual funds), but there are also mortality and expense charges. Read the fine print and don't overpay. Watch out for surrender fees too. Those typically decline over a seven-year period. Personally, I don't like being locked into anything for that long.

Questions To Ask When Purchasing a Fixed Immediate Annuity

1. How much would your monthly payment be for the given amount of money you want to invest?
I like the instant quote feature at www.aigretirementgold.com/vlip/VLIPController?page=RequestaQuote. There are concerns about AIG as the underlying insurer for an annuity right now, but the calculator is helpful in showing you approximately what to expect. You can then compare this to other annuities available.

2. Can you lock in any periods of guaranteed payments even if you die?
That's known as a "term certain." If you're worried that your heirs might not get anything if you die prematurely, look for a "lifetime annuity with a term certain period." Typically you can choose a 10- or 20-year period where your heirs would receive payments if you died before that period is over. But that feature will mean you get a smaller monthly amount for that privilege.

3. Should your annuity cover one life or two?
If you're married, most people prefer that the annuity cover both lives. There are exceptions. If one spouse has a known serious illness, then just cover the life of the healthier spouse. If one spouse is considerably older than the other spouse, you may want to cover just the younger spouse. Annuitizing over one person's life will maximize the annual payment.

If you've made the decision to have an annuity pay out over two lives, you'll have more decisions to make. If you want the spouse to receive the same benefit as when the first-to-die was alive, choose the 100% joint and survivor option. Typically the default is a 50% joint and survivor option for a husband and wife. But that means the survivor has to live on half as much money, which may be difficult. It may mean they have to sell their house or significantly decrease their lifestyle.

4. What is the current fixed rate of return?
When you purchase a fixed annuity, you lock in a fixed rate of return. Make sure you are comfortable with that rate before you sign on the dotted line.

5. *What are the costs?*

Make sure you know how the insurance company issuing the annuity makes its money. You should be able to avoid the mortality and expense charges and underlying investment expenses if you use a fixed annuity. Typically insurers make money on fixed annuities by paying out a bit less than they actually earn on the contribution.

6. *Does the annuity offer inflation protection?*

In my opinion, it's worth taking the time to find an annuity that has inflation protection. This reduces the risk that your payments won't keep up if we have inflation in the future.

7. *What is the financial strength of the insurer?*

After the past few years, we all know that even big companies can fail. So do a little checking—is the insurer issuing your annuity on solid ground? Choose a company that rates in the top tier. Staying with a higher quality company means less unpleasant surprises down the road. As we mentioned before, you can check life insurance ratings by purchasing the annual ratings issue of *The Insurance Forum* at www.theinsuranceforum.com/pages/ratings.html.

Fixed annuities can play an important role in creating a complete retirement strategy. They can help create peace of mind by providing an income stream for life.

Tough Love

After going through one of the roughest years on record in the stock market in 2008, we realized that it was critical to revisit the past retirement projections we'd done for our clients. Asset balances were lower and some expectations for the future had changed. Although our expected returns on asset classes had always been conservative, we wanted to build in even more modest expectations for the future. We also increased the volatility factors in the model to anticipate more bumps in the road going forward.

We knew what we would find: in many cases we would need to talk to our clients about cutting back on what they were spending in retirement and perhaps talk about postponing retirement. This is what I would call tough love. Clients were already upset about losing money. Here we came with more bad news.

But by getting a jump on potential future problems, we hoped to head off more difficulties in the future when it might be even tougher to recover.

Some people always know every penny they spend. But probably more aren't really sure. We encourage everyone to track their spending for at least three months (one year is better) to see just where their money is going. For people in retirement, especially new retirees, this can be very enlightening.

One client said to us recently that he was very grateful for this exercise because they were spending quite a bit more than he had realized. When he was working this was never an issue because more money always came in. But now he was seeing that he had to be more careful about potentially depleting the nest egg too fast.

Case Study: Lessons in Happiness from the Great Depression

My aunt Cynthia is a client and we've had several conversations about spending in retirement. She remembered what my grandmother told her some years after the Great Depression. This is her account.

> "I remember playing in our Victory Garden when I was four years old. This dates me, I know. Now, at 65, I keep remembering my mother's words: 'Hard times will come again,' she'd say. And now I am quite thankful that many of the cost saving habits she taught me (more by example than by words alone) keep popping back into my memories.
>
> When Sue said, 'Ok, you need to watch your spending now,' I know she was telling us (in her always diplomatic and most gentle way), that we should probably refigure our budget. We'd already figured some of that out last spring, but now we began in earnest. Although we've never been really big spenders, we have enjoyed a comfortable life, and I confess we each have our frailties. I, for example, love my techie stuff–couldn't resist the iPod and fell for the iPhone, have more than one computer, like the Wi-Fi things, that sort of weakness. Gary loves his golf games, his books, our Shakespeare theatre outings. We both loved taking our first–and probably our last–cruise in August when we went to Alaska to see the glaciers before (we feared) they possibly melt away.
>
> So yes, we've enjoyed our retirement so far, and interest-

ingly, we expect to continue enjoying it. Financial happiness for us has always just meant having enough to, well, to say 'yes' to really important stuff and 'no' to things that don't matter quite so much. Knowing the difference, of course, is the trick!

We learned early on the difference between 'need' and 'want.' Our parents, who were young adults during the Great Depression, were of course the source of most of that learning. But our own early experiences as young adults–in school, college, graduate school, with young children, surviving the seventies and its inflationary times–also taught us well. But then came the runaway 'good times' of the nineties and the last few years, and like many others, we succumbed more than we care to sometimes admit to spending that far exceeded our 'needs' and wandered dangerously into the land of 'want.'

But did it really satisfy? Living in that land of 'want therefore buy?' I think of the carloads of stuff we've carted off to Goodwill, to the church rummage sale, to the Salvation Army. It's odd, but I'm always so relieved to see it go. Over the past several years, I have come to realize that I neither want nor need much of the stuff I thought I did. Happiness has very little to do with stuff or possessions.

So now, in this time of great national crisis which means for many of us personal trauma and for many more even, personal crisis, I am feeling peculiarly 'ready.' I am ready for change, for re-examination, for major housecleaning, retrenchment, for learning new habits and rediscovering some of the old ones. I am ready.

And I'm betting that many others are ready as well. Wouldn't it be challenging and (I'm almost afraid to write this) fun even to start sharing some of the ways in which we are all rediscovering these roots of true happiness? As a nation, we've been circling issues of energy conservation, recycling, food sources, agricultural practices, borrowing and lending, and many more over the past few years. And as one individual, I've been having fun (yes, I said it) figuring out ways to cut our budget without truly hurting (yet) and–in some wonderfully odd way–I've been enjoying life more.

Here are just a few ways I'm enjoying these changes we've made:

» *We own our home, a modest two-story suburban affair, which, at 2,400 square feet, is probably larger than we really need. And it does cost a lot to heat during Wisconsin winters. But who wants to sell now? Fortunately, we don't have to. Instead, to help with those ever-rising utility bills, we bought two heat-saving drapes and installed them allowing us to keep our thermostat at 58-60 degrees in most of the house, while the area we mostly live in (kitchen and family room) is heated more comfortably by a gas fireplace we can set at 68 degrees. Since I love sleeping in a chilly bedroom, this is no hardship; snuggling down under a comforter is one of life's greatest happinesses.*

» *My friend Sharon inspired me this summer to put up a clothesline. For years, she's been hanging out the laundry. In my go-go life, I thought I didn't have 'time.' Now, of course, I've no excuse, so from May through October at least we can hang our clothes out and let nature's sunshiny breezes do the work. Remembering a childhood filled with helping my mother hang out the family washing has also provided a true happiness. Our latest bill showed we'd cut our gas usage in half from the same period last year.*

» *A few years ago, we replaced our three old toilets with newer ones that use a fraction of the water. The water bill dropped by 20%.*

» *I've always loved to cook. Shopping for and using basic ingredients has always provided me great enjoyment, so I can't claim that this means changing anything. Combining healthy eating with intelligent and economical shopping habits really does make one happier: when we eat better, we feel better, and when we save money, we feel REALLY better! High fiber diets include some nicely inexpensive ingredients: bulk brown rice, dried beans, whole wheat/grain flours, root vegetables. By saving money with these ingredients, one needn't feel guilty about splurging on the fresh fruits and vegetables we also need. Nice result: my blood pressure and cholesterol counts are now lower than ever, and I may be able to avoid prescription medications for either condition. Another savings!*

» *Other healthy–and economical–habits I've been working on: walk with my backpack or shopping cart to the grocery store 1/2 mile away. Take more frequent trips and buy less at a time so this can be done. I get more exercise, and the car uses less fuel.*

» *Speaking of which, we were lucky when we decided three years ago to buy a Prius. It goes without saying that when gas prices went haywire this past summer, we didn't hurt quite as much as we would have with a more conventional car.*

» *Little things add up:*

- *I've just figured out–with my new Medicare status–how to use that mail-in prescription for three-month supplies. Some of the medications–generic–are even free with this option!*

- *Yes, I'm remembering more often to turn out the lights, having already replaced all those old light bulbs with the new kind that uses a fraction of the energy.*

- *Although my children no doubt laugh at me, I use leftovers. I enjoy finding creative ways to use them! Another happiness...*

- *A couple of years ago, I re-taught myself how to sew. During my working years, I did not have time to sew. Now I do, and I'm enjoying making some of my own clothes, learning how to use scraps in quilts, old t-shirts in a duvet cover. Making things, designing things, provides another kind of happiness, and it also saves money.*

- *I love to read, and our public library is a great source of happiness. One does not need to leave a comfortable couch to be transported to other worlds, other lives and new discoveries.*

Discovering ways to save money to live more economically does not make me feel deprived. On the contrary, I feel enriched. Memories flood back, I am grateful. I am especially and keenly aware of how lucky we are: my family, and many who may be reading this, are among the luckiest people in the world. It doesn't take a genius to be aware of the fact that while we are safe and comfortable inside homes we own or nearly own, have plenty of food, are free from true want, many billions of people on our earth do not have any of these blessings. It seems to me that I must always be–every single day–aware of this and thankful for my good fortune and good health. I must do whatever I can not only to practice personal habits of good sense and thrift, but to extend even more generously than ever before our support of church, community, and the larger world."

Health Care Concerns

....

When I started out twenty years ago counseling people about personal finance, I had no idea how often health matters would come up. It's a frequent topic of conversation in client meetings. It might be someone's own health. Or their future health needs. Or a parent's health status. Perhaps the need for assisted living or long-term care.

These issues are a major concern as you plan life transitions. If you retire before age 65 when you may be eligible for Medicare, you'll need to plan for the cost of private health insurance. (At this date, there has been no new legislation on a new federal health plan.)

We all like to think we are invincible, but eventually it occurs to us that we need to plan for the day when we need additional help. Many clients express this as they seek to find a trusted partner to provide continuity for their families.

We've seen a lot of clients make the transition from a single family home to transitional living (a retirement community that offers independent living, assisted living and nursing home care). There are a number of important questions to ask if you are considering that as part of your future.

Health insurance won't pay for long-term care and Medicare only covers the first 100 days if you meet certain conditions. Not everyone can afford long-term care (nursing home) insurance and some won't need it because they can self-insure. But for everyone else, you should at least consider how you would pay for this expense which can cost hundreds of thousands of dollars if you don't have insurance. I know. I watched as both of my grandmothers needed nursing home care in their 90s and the effect that had on the money that eventually went to their children.

If you choose to purchase long-term care coverage, stick with one of the highest-rated insurers for this product. You want them to be around when you need the benefits. Most good policies also cover home health care and that's what most people want for as long as possible.

At Stevens Wealth Management, we've developed a checklist that you can use to evaluate policies:

Long-Term Care Checklist	Company 1	Company 2	Company 3
Name of Insurance Provider			
Financial Rating			
Levels of Care Covered:			
Skilled nursing care?			
Intermediate care?			
Personal/ custodial care?			
Location of Care:			
Home care benefits?			
~ Skilled Care?			
~ Home Health Aides?			
~ Home Modifications?			
Maximum Daily Benefits:			
Nursing Home Care ($)			
Nursing Home Care (# days)			
Home Care ($)			
Home Care (# days/visits)			
Length of Benefit Period (# yrs)			
Lifetime Limits:			
Is there a Lifetime Limit?			
~ Nursing Home Care?			
~ Home Care			
Inflation Protection:			
Inflation Rider available? Type?			
Miscellaneous Features:			
Waiver-of-Premium Feature?			
Guaranteed Renewable?			
Non-Forfeiture Provision?			
Return of Premium Benefit?			
Death Benefit?			
Benefits:			
Elimination Period (days)			
Eligibility Requirements:			
Doctor Certification, Medical Necessity, or ADLs?			
Costs:			
Is Policy Tax-Qualified?			
Monthly Premium?			
Monthly Premium with all Riders and Discounts?			

For additional information, Phyllis Shelton has written a good book that goes into more detail. I've referenced it in Appendix C.

Additional Resources

Retirement planning is a massive topic and we've just scratched the surface today. Even single topics like taxation of retirement assets are quite complex. One book that covers that subject extremely well is Natalie Choate's *Life and Death Planning for Retirement Benefits*. It is very technical, but I refer to it often. Look to her website, www.ataxplan.com for continuing updates.

Other excellent books on retirement planning include Ed Slott's *Your Complete Retirement Planning Road Map*, Harold Evensky & Deena Katz's *Retirement Income Redesigned* and Mary Rowland's *A Commonsense Guide to Your 401(k)*.

Summary

....

Making major life transitions, including retirement, requires upfront planning and analysis. These are complex decisions that are part intellectual and part heart. It's not always easy to put aside your fears and think about what truly makes you happy, but it's critical to taking control of your destiny.

As we've seen, money does not guarantee happiness. I've seen lots of people with more than enough money who are plagued with fears of never having enough. Creativity and freedom seem to be better drivers of happiness. Helping other people almost always contributes to overall happiness.

We're talking about the rest of your life. What have you always wanted to do? How can you get closer to that dream? How can you contribute to someone else's dream? Take the time to give that some thought.

> *"Our deepest fear is not that we are inadequate.*
> *Our deepest fear is that we are powerful beyond measure.*
> *It is our light, not our darkness that most frightens us.*
> *We ask ourselves, 'Who am I to be brilliant, gorgeous,*
> *talented, fabulous?' Actually, who are you not to be?*
> *You are a child of God. Your playing small*
> *does not serve the world. There is nothing*
> *enlightened about shrinking so that other people*
> *won't feel insecure around you. We are all meant to shine,*
> *as children do. We were born to make manifest*
> *the glory of God that is within us. It is not just in some of us;*
> *it is in everyone. And as we let our own light shine,*
> *we unconsciously give other people permission*
> *to do the same. As we are liberated from our own fear,*
> *our presence automatically liberates others."*
> ~ Marianne Williamson

Next, in Chapter Six, we address another part of retirement planning, leaving a legacy. Estate planning is once again a broad topic and I'll show you what I think are the most important concepts to cover.

Chapter Six

The Financial Bridge™

Providing for Loved Ones After You're Gone

Death is a part of life. Although it is frequently feared and often misunderstood, we can't outrun it no matter how much money we have or how pious our lives. Instead, think of it as a bridge between this life and the next.

Many times people only seek professional help when death is involved. Maybe someone passed away from old age. Perhaps there was some sort of accident. Or sometimes it's in preparation of death. Mostly it's just that people are getting older and realize they won't always be able to care for their loved ones the way they have in the past. Or sometimes they know that they are on borrowed time.

We talk about estate planning—how to make sure your assets get to the people and causes you love and that you minimize tax while you're at it. To me, estate planning is really about love. It's less about what you've accumulated and more about who you want to have what. Perhaps it's a family heirloom that should go to someone who will appreciate and care for it.

Perhaps it's a loyal family pet that deserves just the right home when you're gone. And yes, it's about money. What do you want that money to do? That needs to be formalized in legal documents.

Dealing with Death

Sometimes clients come to us because of a tragedy. I've worked with many trauma survivors over the years—people who have lost loved ones in plane crashes, car accidents, even 9/11. One of these stories involved one of my best friend's sister. She had just lost her husband in a rafting accident and was trying to raise their thirteen year-old daughter.

> *"I'll be forever grateful that Kay referred me to you after my husband died ten years ago. We've managed to make the small amount of life insurance benefits grow to support Cara's college and graduate school and enable me to retire at age 54. I've felt that with your careful stewardship and advice, I've been able to focus on family and getting on with my life rather than spending time worrying about a lack of abundance."*

Sue leads a satisfying life and has kept her focus on what she loves—her daughter. We worked through many issues including eventually leaving her full-time teaching job. Her daughter is now just about through college, has bought her first home and is engaged to a wonderful man. Sue has also found someone that she enjoys spending time with and who is a joy in her life.

Dealing with people after a traumatic loss takes a gentle hand. Often it takes a year to just work through all the issues that emerge. If you are ever in this situation, please take your time. No one should rush you.

Why All This Talk About Death?

Because you ask for it—over and over. You've figured out there is no way around the fact that we leave this life for another and part of putting your money where your heart is includes where that money goes after death.

Death and money have historically been taboo subjects. And yet, almost everywhere I go, they are becoming more frequent topics of conversation. At a recent dinner party, people talked about whether they had written their own obituaries yet. And which retirement community they had put a deposit down on. These people were not the very old—a step away from death. They were in the prime of life.

My mom recently asked me to speak to her church group. I asked her what topic she'd like me to prepare—recovering from the market meltdown? Leaving a legacy? No, she said, bring *The Survivor's Checklist*. Everybody always loves that. They send it to each other when someone dies.

And apparently she's right. At a recent "Bogleheads" conference (an annual gathering of participants of the www.bogleheads.org website), one woman told the story of how she lost her husband and how *The Survivor's Checklist* article helped her through the process. I was moved and honored that I could help in this way.

So there's no sense pretending it's not going to happen. Instead, let's talk about the issues that are important to all of us—what happens to a lifetime of cherished memories and loves when we cross that bridge to a better life.

The Financial Bridge™

I can't tell you how many meetings I've been in where one of the primary concerns is that the spouse who is more financially involved is very concerned he or she set up a relationship with an advisor for the other spouse long before either one is seriously ill. They are looking for someone they can trust to be there for their families after they are gone. They want to know that their wishes will be honored and that their affairs are in order. So we think of our firm as a Financial Bridge™ for our clients. And it seemed logical to put together a series of exercises and templates to help you gather your thoughts about these important issues.

Here's what most people need to do:

» Prepare estate documents
» Coordinate beneficiary designations and account titling so that legal documents work the way you intend them to
» Take the necessary steps to make sure your family, including your animals, will have the financial and emotional support they need after you are gone
» Get organized so that people can find the relevant documents they need to settle your estate
» Leave a checklist for survivors that walks them through what they'll need to do even if they are in a state of shock
» Write down what you want to happen at your memorial service including what the obituary should say and what music you love

Put it all in a binder, give a copy to someone you trust and you'll have completed The Financial Bridge™.

Procrastination is common. Most people find it hardest to decide who should care for their children or settle their estate or manage their money once they pass away. My advice? Just get it done. Choose somebody and know that you can always change it later. Then be on the lookout for someone with the qualities that you now know you need for your loved ones.

An Overview of Estate Planning

If you don't already have estate documents, chances are you'll need them. If you do have documents, you may need to update them if they are over ten years old. To help you prepare for this, we will outline what you need to know about these types of documents.

Wills, Trusts and Everything Else

There are lots of good reasons to put an estate plan in place. Sure, you want to save on taxes and pass more money to your heirs. But you also want to have some say about who's going to get those assets and at what point in time.

You may be surprised to learn that often times, very little actually passes to your heirs by will. If you have retirement plans or insurance policies, they pass by beneficiary designation. If you haven't checked on who your beneficiaries are recently, make that a top priority.

If you hold assets inside a trust, they pass according to the provisions of the trust. There are lots of kinds of trusts that we'll discuss more in-depth shortly.

If you own your home in joint tenancy with rights of survivorship or by tenants of the entirety, that property passes to the survivor regardless of what your will says. Only if you are tenants-in-common can you pass your share of the property by will.

Just about everything else passes by will. Typically, that can be things like a car or an individual checking account. It can also be personal property like family heirlooms or jewelry.

Assets that pass by will go through a legal process called probate. This court proceeding validates your will and starts the process of distributing your estate. Final expenses and estate taxes are often paid out of the probate estate. You want to make sure that your heirs have enough liquidity to cover those costs without having to sell something you never intended for them to part with.

A Taxing Matter

Estate taxes can be one of the most onerous taxes your heirs may encounter. Currently estate tax rates are higher than income tax rates. Take a look at how rates change over the next couple years. The "exemption equivalent" is the amount you can pass to your heirs estate tax-free.

Year	Exemption Amount	Highest Rate
2009	$3,500,000	45%
2010	Estate tax repealed	0%
2011	$1,000,000	55%

As you can see from the above table, in 2010 the estate tax is entirely repealed. Unless Congress makes changes, the estate tax will reappear in 2011 using the amounts and rates that were in effect in 2001.

At present when an heir receives property from an estate, the property takes a "stepped-up basis," protecting the heir from capital gains tax on appreciation that occurred prior to the estate settlement. Under the new scenario in 2010, when there is no estate tax, heirs will receive limited step-ups which could expose more of the inheritance to capital gains tax.

It is not only possible, but likely, that prior to 2010 Congress will make changes to the situations described above.

A Matter of Trusts

Living Trusts

A living trust is created during your lifetime as opposed to a "testamentary" trust which is created when you die. You won't save any estate tax by using a living trust.

The living trust becomes your primary estate document and may control several other testamentary trusts built into it. A "pour-over" will is frequently a companion document that deposits probated assets into the trust. From there provisions are made about how the money is to be distributed.

A living trust does not go through probate. That means your heirs can get money almost immediately after your death without waiting for everything to go through probate.

A living trust also provides protection during your lifetime. If you are incapacitated, you can name someone to manage your affairs (a successor trustee) until you are able to resume your trustee duties.

If you change your mind about any provisions in your living trust, you can revise your documents. Nothing is carved in stone.

It won't do you any good to set up a living trust and then forget to fund it. You'll need to retitle your brokerage accounts, at a minimum, to reflect the new ownership. This is relatively simple to do.

Family Trusts

Family trusts can save your heirs a lot of money. They are called by several different names: a credit shelter or credit equivalent trust or sometimes a "B" trust. Whatever you call this trust, it may save hundreds of thousands of dollars in estate tax.

Here's how a family trust works:

1. You set up a family trust within your living trust or will. At your death, it becomes active.

2. Your living trust or will specifies that the family trust is to be funded with whatever the exemption equivalent amount is at that time. (Remember the exemption equivalent is how much can pass to your heirs estate tax-free.)

3. The money going into the family trust is taxed, but Uncle Sam gives you a credit (the "unified" credit) that offsets the tax. So you don't owe a dime.

4. Your spouse has access to the interest and principal as needed for their health, maintenance, education and welfare.

5. At your spouse's death, whatever is left in the trust (which may have grown to a larger amount than it started with) passes free and clear to your heirs, without paying any more estate tax.

Marital Trusts

A generation or two ago many patriarchal families used marital trusts. A marital trust sets up provisions for the management of money for the spouse's benefit. In many cases nowadays, assets are left outright to the spouse. He or she is free to hire a financial advisor to help them manage the money.

You can pass an unlimited amount to your spouse both during your lifetime and at death without paying any gift or estate tax. There is an unlimited marital deduction that allows you to pass assets to your spouse at death without paying any estate tax. But watch out: if you do that, you may be setting your spouse up for a huge estate tax at his or her death.

If you decide you want to leave a marital trust, interest must be paid out to the spouse at least quarterly. Principal may also be paid out for health, education, maintenance and support.

You also can choose from less restrictive to more restrictive versions of a marital trust.

Less restrictive

If you don't want to leave assets outright to your spouse, but you don't want to be unduly restrictive, you can create a marital trust with a general power of appointment. This allows your spouse to leave the assets in the marital trust to whoever he or she chooses.

More restrictive

If you want control over the marital trust assets after your spouse dies, you can create a Qualified Terminal Interest Property (QTIP) trust. This is often used in families where a second marriage has created a blended family with children from prior marriages.

Children's Trusts

A children's trust can specify that a pool of money is made available for education expenses and support until the children are through college. After that, you can specify that a portion be paid out at various ages. By doing that, if the child spends the first installment foolishly, he or she will have another chance to do something responsible with the next distribution of assets.

Special Needs Trusts

Sometimes loved ones with disabilities need additional protection. This type of trust supplements any government assistance they may be eligible for. It's a complex area and you should seek out a professional for guidance.

Charitable Trusts

Once you've achieved a significant level of wealth, you may find yourself wanting to do more philanthropic giving. There are many ways of structuring this from a tax perspective that can be advantageous. There are charitable lead trusts, charitable remainder trusts, private foundations and so forth. How you structure this type of trust depends on when you want to receive a tax deduction, if you want money to come to you during your lifetime or if you want anything to go to your heirs ultimately.

Choose Your Executors and Trustees Wisely

Executors

An executor or executrix handles the administration of closing up your estate. That person needs to be able to work with an attorney, accountant and/or financial advisor to complete the necessary paperwork and ultimately distribute the assets. You can name an individual and/or an institution to act as an executor (or they can act as co-executors).

Some characteristics to look for in an executor are sensitivity, competence, an understanding of the needs and circumstances of the beneficiaries, knowledge of the nature, value, and extent of your assets, experience in the administration of estates, business and investment experience, familiarity with your business, ability and willingness to serve, geographic proximity to your beneficiaries and the estate's assets, lack of any conflict of interest, integrity and loyalty.

Trustees

You'll also need to give some thought to who should be your trustee if you set up a trust of any kind. This person and/or institution will need to monitor and oversee the distribution of income and principal as necessary to your heirs. They need to be compassionate, yet follow the instructions in the trust document.

Characteristics to look for in a trustee are availability, impartiality, lack of conflict of interest, financial security, investment and/or business sophistication, accounting and tax-planning expertise, recordkeeping and reporting ability, knowledge of and sensitivity to beneficiaries and their circumstances, reasonable fees, solid decision-making abilities, overall competence and integrity.

Powers of Attorney

Powers of attorney are an essential tool for managing disability. They are inexpensive and simple to set up. There are two kinds of powers of attorney:

1. Health Care Power

You choose an agent to act on your behalf should you be unable to make your own health care decisions. This person needs to know if you wish to be kept alive on life support or if you choose to forgo all medical means available. Here are some typical options to choose from:

> » I do not want my life to be prolonged, nor do I want life-sustaining treatment to be provided or continued if my agent believes the burdens of the treatment outweigh the expected benefits. I want my agent to consider the relief of suffering, the expense involved, and the quality as well as the possible extension of my life in making decisions concerning life-sustaining treatment.

> » I want my life to be prolonged, and I want life-sustaining treatment to be provided or continued unless I am in a coma which my attending physician believes to be irreversible, in accordance with reasonable medical standards at the time of reference. If and when I have suffered an irreversible coma, I want life-sustaining treatment to be withheld or discontinued.

> » I want my life to be prolonged to the greatest extent possible without regard to my condition, the chances I have for recovery, or the cost of the procedures.

2. Durable Power for Property

You'll also need an agent to act on your behalf if you are incapacitated and can't sign a tax return, make investment decisions, make gifts or handle other financial matters.

Gifting Strategies

Once you feel that you have more than enough money to cover your own lifetime needs, you may want to think about gifting to family, friends and/or charities.

You can give up to $13,000 per person per year (in 2009) to as many people as you'd like without paying any gift tax. You can give an unlimited amount to charity per year without paying gift tax and potentially receive a tax deduction in return.

If you give more than the annual exclusion ($13,000), you may still not have to pay gift tax because you have a lifetime credit that allows you to gift up to $1,000,000 in total assets without owing gift tax.

A Love Story

Once you understand the basics about estate documents, you can tackle the hard part. Who and what do you care about? That's where you want your money and belongings to go. It's not enough to leave verbal instructions. That's how family feuds get started. You need to put your intentions in writing, preferably through an estate attorney.

When you boil it down, it's all about love. We recently lost a dear client who had been with us for a long time. I came into work one morning, in the midst of the market meltdown, and my staff hurried to tell me "Marv has died." Understandably I was filled with emotion.

I called his widow who I had grown to know over the years. Her first words to me were "I was adored." That will stay with me forever. That kind of love inspires me and is why I want to play the role we do in helping our clients through this tough life transition. I continue to feel the love between this husband and wife and I want to help make the financial part of this as seamless as possible.

A few months after Marv's death, I went out to visit with his widow. We had a deep discussion about what happens next for her including how to handle her own estate planning. We went out for lunch, toasted Marv and became even closer than we were before. This is the kind of joy that makes financial planning so rewarding.

Here are some questions and guidelines to help you think through how you want to handle these decisions.

Who or What Do You Love?

	What Should Happen?	Financial Support
My Kids	Who should act as guardian? When should they have access to money? Multiple ages?	Who should act as trustee of the funds? How much should you leave and for what purpose?
My Spouse:		
~ Taxable Assets	These will be used first to pay taxes and final expenses	
~ Retirement Funds	Your spouse can rollover your plans. Your other heirs can stretch out benefits over their lifetimes. Charities won't owe tax on the donation.	
My Animals	Who will care for your pets? Will they have to be split up? Who will make end of life decisions?	Will you leave assets to pay for their care?
My Family Heirlooms	Who in the family is responsible enough to care for family treasures? Leave a written or video commentary explaining who the people are in your longtime family photos.	Should you leave money for upkeep?
My Car, Golf Clubs, Cello, Jewelry	Unless you've titled these in the name of your trust, you need to say in your will or addendum where these special items should go.	
My Charities	Which organizations have made a difference in your life?	How should you allocate your money between people and institutions?

Coordinating Beneficiary Designations and Titling

You may have the best estate documents in the world, but if you don't have your accounts set up to flow into them, you've wasted your money. This is where it helps to understand how assets flow at death.

Here are a few things to think about in this process:

» If you have a living trust, make sure your accounts are held in your name as trustee of your trust. If they are in your individual name, they may not flow to your trust.

» Fund your trusts. This is typically done by putting assets in the name of the trust.

» Check your current beneficiary designations on retirement accounts, company insurance and other company benefits, and outside life insurance policies. Be especially cautious with old policies or benefits. This is frequently where we'll find parents (who are now deceased) or former spouses listed. Your will or trust does not override beneficiary designations.

» If you are married, try to equalize your estate to minimize taxes. In 2009, each spouse can pass $3.5 million to heirs at death free of estate tax. You may want to think about re-titling the house in the name of the spouse with fewer assets.

Writing Your Obituary

Not everyone is going to want to rush right out and do this, but I am seeing more and more people express an interest. So let's just tackle it.

In the fall of 2009, I had college and graduate school reunions within weeks of each other. Each one wanted a short written blurb about what I've done with my life since school. It occurs to me that these aren't that different from an obituary. One way or another, you'll probably need to succinctly sum up your life.

Key Elements

Getting started is the hardest part. Here are some key elements you may wish to incorporate:

» **Occupation:** Make it interesting. You don't have to be listed as "Accountant." You can be "Top Chicago Area Forensic Accountant."

» **Funeral and burial arrangements** (See p.114 for thoughts on things to consider.)

» **Important relationships:** Who have you loved? Parents? Spouses? Children? Teachers? Animals?

» **Achievements:** What do you consider to be your greatest lifetime achievements? It doesn't have to be that you are a PhD in economics and won the Nobel Prize. It can be that you made the best apple pie in McHenry County and your kitchen was always open for the people you loved.

» **Anything else that matters to you**

Example

Henry Washburn, Talented Asheville-Area Clarinetist

Henry "Hank" Washburn [*age*], much loved principal clarinetist of the Brevard Music Festival, died of [*cause of death*] [*date*] at [*place of death*]. Mr. Washburn lived in Buncombe County for the past twenty years and taught children of all ages at the Asheville Music School.

Mr. Washburn was born in Akron, Ohio July 27, 1946 and leaves a sister, Karen Williams, who lives in Philadelphia, PA; an uncle, Russell Knight of Santa Fe, NM.; and a great aunt, Charlotte Beckes of Lima, Ohio. A sister, Rachel, and a brother, Michael, predeceased Hank. His beloved cat Spectacles will be cared for by his best friend Tom Hunter.

In high school, Hank was selected to perform with the New York Wind Ensemble. He studied clarinet at Northwestern University, where he was a member of their Symphony Orchestra and their Symphonic Wind Ensemble. He was much loved for his sparkling eyes and his mischievous sense of humor. Henry toured with many well-known musicians including Frank Sinatra, Sammy Davis Jr. and Liza Minnelli. He appeared briefly in the film *The Soloist*.

Hank considered his greatest achievement to be giving his full attention to the people or cause that he was presented with each moment of his life. Those people will never forget him.

A memorial service celebrating Hank's life will be announced by public invitation and held during the week ending [*date*].
In lieu of flowers, charitable contributions may be made to the Washburn Family Scholarship Fund and mailed to [*address*].

Last Wishes

....

Beyond the formal estate documents and the notice for the paper, there are a number of decisions that need to be made about how to celebrate your life. So many times family and friends really don't know what you would want and how you would choose to be remembered. So do this for them. Here's what they want to know:

» **Burial or Cremation:** What do you want? Is there a particular funeral home you'd prefer or location where you'd like to be buried or for your ashes to be spread? Remember that your loved ones need time to grieve. I've seen many situations where loved ones keep ashes at home for some time before they are ready to scatter them. This is a very personal process and everyone needs to find what they are most comfortable with.

» **Memorial Service:** Do you prefer a church or somewhere else? What kind of music or flowers would you prefer? Is there anyone you'd like to speak? What stories would you like someone to tell? Are there poems or readings that are especially meaningful to you? Which photos would you like to have there?

» **Letters to Special People:** Are there things you want to say? If possible, try to say them in person before you're gone. If that's not possible, write a letter and express your hopes and wishes. Don't use this as an excuse to take out your frustrations. Keep it positive!

» **Letters of Instruction:** If you have children or animals, write down what their favorite toys are, their favorite foods, any special treats they love. Think about how to help the next caregiver make a smooth transition. Remember children and animals grieve too. Take this approach with any special situation you have that merits additional commentary.

» **Food and Drink:** Many people need to have some time to gather to comfort each other, tell stories and remember the person who has died. Where would you like for them to get together? Is there a special place you remember that would be appropriate?

I know many of you are very conscientious and want to do a good job of planning. But don't feel you need to have all the answers. It's perfectly fine to say "Janie, you pick a place for the meal." Just write down those things that you have a strong preference about.

Sacred Music

Being a musician myself, let me give you a few pointers about choosing music for a memorial or funeral service. First, choose music that is beautiful to you. Beautiful music is appropriate at any sacred occasion, be it a wedding or funeral or something else. Second, choose instrumentalists or vocalists that can perform professionally. (You can also use CDs if live music isn't possible.) In general, don't ask someone really close to you to perform because this can be an extremely emotional occasion. But there are always exceptions: sometimes someone close will really want to participate.

Here are some suggestions for music:

» Faure, *Pie Jesu* from Requiem, Op. 48 or Pavane, Op. 50
» Edgar, 'Nimrod' from Enigma Variations, Op. 36
» J.S. Bach, *Largo* from Concerto to Two Violins and Strings, BWV 1043
» Massenet, 'Le dernier sommeil de la Vierge' from La Vierge
» Franck, *Panis Angelicus*
» Mahler, *Adagietto* from Symphony No. 5
» Grieg, 'Death of Ase' from Peer Gynt Suite No. 1, Op. 46

Animal Grace

Now let's turn our attention to our beloved animal companions. Can you ever really have complete peace of mind until you know you've made provisions to take care of those you love the most? Of course your will or trust specifies what should happen to protect your children and spouse. But what about your faithful companions? The four-leggeds or feathered friends who never run out of love and companionship?

Most people assume someone will take their pets after they die. Maybe a relative or a friend. But the rising numbers of animals who have no recourse but a shelter tell a different story.

There are six primary reasons why animals go to shelters:

1. The owner doesn't have the time or money to care for the pet.
2. Behavioral problems with the pet which can be from a lack of proper training.
3. Disputes between landlords and tenants.
4. Owner cannot afford cost of vet care for a sick pet.
5. Family issues like a new baby, allergies, divorce.
6. Lost pet (shelters typically only hold the pet 3-to-5 days before offering them for adoption, euthanizing them or sending them to a research lab).

The high unemployment rate is a major factor in recent surges at animal shelters. For example, the Anderson County Humane Society in South Carolina has seen about 75 animals a day dropped off recently because owners can no longer afford to feed their pets. I recently adopted a new pet and was stunned at the overwhelming number of animals at my local shelter. Clearly the economy is taking a toll on so many of us. So you may want to identify a pet care giver who can also be a foster family if you find yourself in hard economic circumstances.

The elderly frequently are faced with difficult choices regarding their animal companions. They may encounter health issues or financial circumstances that necessitate assistance to keep their pets safe and comfortable. There are a handful of organizations that are committed to helping the elderly keep their pets should they need to move into institutional care (see Resources on p.121) or should they not have the funds to continue paying for animal care.

Have You Considered?

According to the 2009-2010 National Pet Owners Survey, 62% of U.S. households own a pet. That's 71.4 million homes. Dogs lead in popularity with 45.6%, but cats follow closely with 38.2%. Multiple pet families are common. There are 93.6 million cats owned by Americans and 77.5 million dogs.

We spend $45.4 billion (an estimate for 2009) on our pets. That goes toward food, vet visits, supplies, grooming, boarding, etc. But how many of you have actually included language in your estate documents specifying their care? Based on my own informal poll, very few.

Studies show animals not only provide an enormous source of joy and love, but can also play an important role in reducing human health care costs. Here are some of the many proven benefits:

» People with pets are less lonely
» People with pets recover more quickly from illness
» Living with pets can help lower blood pressure
» Recovering heart attack patients live longer when they have a pet
» Alzheimer's patients with pets have fewer anxious outbursts
» Pets encourage movement and exercise
» Pets help decrease depression and anxiety

Another study by the American Animal Hospital Association (U.S. and Canada) reports the following on human-animal bonds:

» 83% adopt pets for companionship
» 44% adopt to keep another pet company
» 66% prepare special pet food

» Of those that have a will, only 27% have included provisions for their pets

» 37% talk to their pets on the phone or answering machine

» 52% provide more exercise for their pets than they do for themselves

» 70% consider their pets as children and seek a very high level of care for their pets

Protecting Your Pet in a Disaster

Many of you have readily available disaster supplies in the event of an emergency. But have you included provisions for your pet? Here's what you should have:

» One week's supply of food and water
» A portable food and water bowl
» A leash, collar (and perhaps a spare)
» Nylon cord or rope
» Extra ID tags
» Swiss Army knife
» Waterproof flashlight and fresh batteries
» Portable carrier
» Health records
» Waterproof blanket and perhaps a tarp
» Recent photos of your pets in case they get lost
» Waterproof matches
» First-aid kit
» Pet toys

What You Should Do

You can't leave the care of your loyal companions to chance. Follow these steps to ensure they have the love and care they deserve:

1. Choose a "pet guardian"

If something happened to you, temporary or permanent, who should care for your pet? If you have multiple pets, do you want them to stay together? Does the person you have in mind have room for multiple pets? Do they have pets of their own? Do they have the financial ability to care for all of them?

Once you decide on who you'd like, talk to them. Make sure everyone is on the same page. Make sure your pets get to know this person long before you'd need to rely on them. Observe how they get along.

Make sure you also choose contingent pet guardians. Despite your best planning efforts, unexpected things can happen.

2. Decide on financial assistance

According to the APPA National Pet Owners Survey, it costs about $1,400 a year to care for a dog on average and about $1,000 for a cat. That covers vet care, food, boarding, grooming, vitamins, treats and toys. Dogs live on average for 12-to-13 years and cats for 12-to-18 years. But that can vary quite a bit depending on the breed and the lifestyle.

If you decide to provide financial assistance to your caregiver, you can set up provisions in a trust to ensure this happens after your death. Be sure to fund your trust appropriately. This means setting up an account in the name of your trust and moving assets into it. Those assets can then be invested any way you choose.

3. Add language to your trust document to provide for your pets' care

Your attorney is the best person to help you draft just the right provisions for what you want, but here is some sample language as an example:

> While any of my pets are alive the trustee may pay so much of the net income and principal as the trustee considers advisable for the maintenance and welfare of my pets which I own at the time of my death. The trustee shall make payments to the individuals caring for my pets for pet food, pet sitters, veterinary bills and any other expenses that are appropriate for the comfort and care of my pets. I direct that my trustees take into account the manner of care that I have provided for my pets during my lifetime.
>
> I direct that my pets be placed in a single private home with one (or more) individuals known to me during my life. The residence should provide for my pets in a similar manner of care and living atmosphere provided during my life. I specifically direct that my pets not be placed in a shelter. The trustees of my trust shall immediately make arrangements for the continual care of my pets in my residence until placement has been completed.

Then you can go on to say what you want to happen to the remaining assets after your pets have all lived out their natural lives.

Do not assume the people you choose as beneficiaries for your assets are the best people to care for your animals. Do not assume the people you choose to care for your pets should also manage the money in the trust (you can name a separate trustee to manage the assets). You may also want to alert your vet to your wishes.

4. Write instructions for your caregiver

Provide a complete historical and medical record for each pet. Here's what you should document:

Pet's Name	
Breed/Color/Distinguishing Marks	
Date of Birth	
Place of Adoption	
Location of Pedigree Papers	
Favorite Toys	
Vet Contact Info	
Medical Issues/Medication Instructions	
Pet's Friends (people and/or animals)	
Designated Caregiver and Contact Info	
Feeding Instructions	

Do this for each animal.

5. Alert emergency workers to your pets

Consider carrying something in your wallet that alerts emergency workers that you have pets at home. This should include a contact to call that can care for your pets if you are incapacitated. This is especially important if you live alone. Make sure your care-taker has access to your home and the written instructions above.

Some people also put a small sign in a window at home that lets emergency workers know there are pets in the house. This would alert police and/or fire fighters that they need to make sure your pets are safe in an emergency.

Summary

When you take on the care of an animal's life, you are rewarded with end-less love, play and affection. You also take on responsibility to keep that animal safe and comfortable for its lifetime. It's more than a fair exchange. Act now to put in place the provisions that will legalize your intentions in the spirit of animal grace.

Resources

Eden Alternative (www.edenalt.org)
Helping the elderly by advocating plants, animals and regular visits by children in long-term care facilities.

Lollypop Farm (www.lollypop.org)
Provides financial assistance to the elderly so that they can keep pets in their homes. A Pet Food Bank is maintained that can provide emergency aid.

For further reading:
All My Children Wear Fur Coats
Peggy R. Hoyt, Legacy Planning Partners, Oviedo, Florida.

Getting Your Affairs in Order

Aside from Woody Allen, most of us probably don't spend a lot of time thinking about our own mortality. And that's probably a good thing – up to a point. Of course, we're all going to die at some point, and one of the kindest things we can do for the loved ones we leave behind is to provide them with explicit documentation of all they'll need to follow our last wishes.

Use the following template to guide your loved ones through what will be a most difficult transition.

Who To Contact

Role	Name	Phone Number	E-mail Address
Financial Advisor			
Attorney			
Accountant			
Funeral Director			
Spiritual Director			
Family			
Friends			
Employer			
Other			

Important Documents

Types of Documents	Where Are They Located?
Legal Documents - Wills, Trusts, Powers of Attorney	
Financial Bridge™	
Net Worth Statement	
Real Estate Deeds	
Marriage Certificate	
Tax Returns	
Safe Deposit Box -Which Bank? Where is the Key?	
Car Title	
Military Records	
Loan Documents	
Prepaid Funeral Paperwork	

Insurance Policies

Company	Location	Approximate Value	Beneficiaries

Company Benefits

Type	Contact	Approximate Value	Online Access URL	User ID/Password
Stock Options				
Restricted Stock				
Deferred Comp				

Accounts | Taxable

Type	Locations	Account Number	Approximate Value	Online Access URL	User ID/ Password
Brokerage					
Checking					
CDs					

Accounts | Retirement

Type	Locations	Account Number	Approximate Value	Beneficiary	Online Access URL	User ID/ Password
IRA						
401(k)						
Annuity						

Accounts | Kids

Type	Locations	Account Number	Approximate Value	Online Access URL	User ID/ Password
529					
UTMA/UGMA					

The Stevens Wealth Management
Survivor's Checklist

Losing a loved one is one of the most difficult things any of us will have to endure in our lifetimes. The experience is made all the more difficult by the myriad of paperwork and red tape that the survivor must wade through at precisely the moment in their life when they're most ill-equipped to deal with it.

With that in mind, here's a brief checklist that covers what a survivor needs to do in order to navigate this emotional time.

1. Call your trusted advisors.

They are there to help. Even if the death is expected, you will probably be in a state of shock. Your advisors can gently help you prioritize what needs to be done.

2. Make funeral or memorial service arrangements.

Sometimes people set up pre-paid and pre-arranged instructions. See if there are any such directives. If not, work with the funeral home or spiritual institution you choose to make all the arrangements including submitting the obituary, setting a time for a service, making burial or cremation arrangements.

3. Gather relevant documents.

If you're lucky, someone will leave you a Financial Bridge™ to help you know where everything is. Start by locating all essential papers that may include the following:

- » A copy of the will, and, if applicable, trusts
- » Recent statements for any IRAs, 401(k)s, investment accounts, bank accounts, and pension plans
- » Insurance policies
- » Social Security numbers
- » Military discharge papers, if applicable
- » Marriage license
- » Divorce decrees from previous marriages, if applicable
- » Children's birth certificates

» Death certificate (plan on needing two dozen or so copies)
» Company benefit records

4. File for life insurance benefits.

Most insurers will pay out a death benefit within a week or so of receiving a copy of the deceased's death certificate. In most cases, they'll place it in an account earning a nominal amount of interest, which will allow you to focus elsewhere for the time being.

> » If you cannot find the insurance policies, MIB Solutions, an insurance membership corporation (www.mib.com), will help you find it for a fee. Alternatively, the American Council of Life Insurers (www.acli.com) offers tips on finding a missing policy.

5. Contact the deceased's employer.

Most employers will quickly pay any wages owed and unused vacation or sick time. If they died on the job, you may also be eligible for accidental death and dismemberment benefits.

You should also talk to the human resources department about health insurance benefits if you were enrolled through the deceased's employer. At a minimum, spouses may be able to retain the coverage for up to 36 months through COBRA.

6. Check your cash reserves.

Between funeral costs and a host of other unexpected expenses – in addition to your normal expenses – you can find that you're burning through cash more quickly that you anticipated, so it's a good idea to make sure that you have a bit more in your cash reserves than normal. Six-to-eight months of living expenses should be sufficient to buy you the time you need to get your legs under you. To fund this, you might transfer a portion of the life insurance benefits to your savings account. Some insurance companies will even provide you with a debit card you can use to draw on the benefit.

7. Consider government death benefits.

Widows or widowers may be eligible for Social Security at age 60. Families with dependent children under 18 are also eligible for survivors' benefits. Visit www.ssa.gov to determine what you're eligible for.

Military veterans are eligible for a free burial in a national cemetery. The Veterans Administration will also provide a flag, headstone, and financial assistance. If you choose to have burial in a private cemetery, the VA will also arrange to have a military funeral conducted at the gravesite.

8. Consider retirement plan options.

If you were the primary beneficiary of your spouse's IRA, and he or she was the original owner, you may transfer the plan's assets into an IRA in your name. Doing so will prevent you from having to take any distributions from it until you turn 70 1/2. If your spouse was not the original owner, or if you do not want to transfer it to an IRA in your name, you may be able to take a distribution from it without having to pay any early withdrawal penalties. You will owe income taxes on any distribution, however. You're also able to roll your spouse's 401(k) plan directly into an IRA in your name. Some employers will permit you to keep the assets in the company's plan, if you choose. Doing so may allow you to tap those assets earlier if you are considerably younger than your spouse while avoiding early withdrawal penalties.

If you are the beneficiary of a retirement plan, but not the spouse, you cannot roll over the plan to your own IRA. You can set up a beneficiary IRA account and you will have to take required minimum distributions (for both traditional and Roth IRAs). You can also "cash out" the plan, but then you would owe tax on the whole distribution.

Consulting with a trusted financial advisor may help you determine which option is best for you.

9. Settle the estate.

The will names an executor, who will handle the administrative duties of distributing the estate, and you'll be working very closely with them during this process. If you have a safe-deposit box, make sure that you and the executor take an inventory of it.

You should also consider enlisting an estate attorney to help you file any estate tax returns and final income tax returns that are required. The estate tax return must be filed within nine months of the date of death, and the final income tax return must be filed by April 15th of the year following the date of death.

10. Take care of the miscellany.

You've now taken care of the most immediate needs, but a few more issues remain. At some point, you'll have to re-title all of your assets, such as your house, car, savings accounts, etc. You'll also want to change the names on your checking accounts and credit cards. In each case, you'll need to make your request in writing, and enclose a copy of the death certificate.

You should change the beneficiaries of your own life insurance policies and retirement accounts if the deceased was previously named on these. Now is also a good time to revisit your own will and any trusts, to make sure that they're up-to-date.

11. Take a fresh look at spending needs.

You've been through a lot. Once you get past the first several months, it may make sense to meet with your advisor to re-evaluate how much you can spend going forward. It may be more or less than you did in the past. Your advisor can help you understand what you own, what you owe and how to make your money last throughout your lifetime.

12. Create a memorial.

Sometimes one of the most healing things to do is create a small memorial in their honor. It needn't be anything lavish; something as simple as a garden in the corner of your yard or a small paver in a walkway with their name on it can serve as a tangible tribute to their life, and to the role they played in yours.

Above all else, recognize your own emotional needs throughout this process. You're going through one of the darkest phases of your life, so by all means enlist the help of your friends and family as you negotiate your way through the things that a loved one's death makes necessary so that they can help you get back on your feet. It will help both you and them get through this difficult period.

Have an Open Discussion

At this point, you should be ready to get your estate documents in place and complete all sections of the Financial Bridge™. But your work is not complete without some kind of discussion with your loved ones. I know no one really wants to do this and your loved ones may protest. Nonetheless, talking to your loved ones about what you plan to do with your estate is the best way to eliminate any confusion and surprises when the time comes.

Tell your family what you're planning to do, and the logic behind it. If you own family heirlooms that will be much sought after, seek to negotiate a reasonable compromise with your potential heirs so that their grief won't be mixed with hard feelings – the last thing you would want your death to do is cause a rift in your family. And most important, make sure your children's potential guardian is comfortable with your wishes, and make sure that they have (with your help) the financial means necessary to provide the care that your children will need.

Although it's not any fun to contemplate, taking these steps is a final gift you can provide your loved ones – one which they will be eternally grateful for having received. And once you've taken care of the business of preparing for your death, you can move on to the much happier business of getting on with your life.

Start Now

It's never going to seem like the right time to start this process. So just get it done. It doesn't have to be perfect and you don't need to have all the answers right now.

Set up a network of people you trust as you establish your own Financial Bridge™. Put some thought into how you want to be remembered, organize all important information in a binder, give it to someone to hold on your behalf or let them know where to find it.

After all, to the well-organized mind,
death is but the next great adventure.
~J.K. Rowling

Chapter Seven

A Matter of Trust

Choosing a Financial Partner

M ost of us enter the financial advisory business because we genuinely want to help. Sure, there are some bad apples. Bernie Madoff comes to mind. But what I want you to know is that there are people out there who are not out to just sell you products. There are people who will be on your side, think about what's in your best interest and who want you to succeed.

Finding the right person to work with takes some homework. You need to know the right questions to ask. You need to trust your gut. If the relationship doesn't feel right, you're never going to develop the kind of partnership you'll need to face really tough decisions at times.

We listen. We give words of assurance. We serve.
When we put the phone down, who feels better? The client does,
we hope. But we do, too! And when we reflect on what took place,
we understand more clearly who we really are and what
we have to offer others. The best way we can fulfill our highest
wellness potential is through service to others. Success in life is
measured not by longevity or wealth or honors or power. Helping
others becomes a natural way of expressing compassion.
~ Greg Anderson, *The 22 Non-Negotiable Laws of Wellness*

Ask the Right Questions

The National Association of Personal Financial Advisors (NAPFA) is a group of fee-only advisors. I'm a member. I think they hold advisors to a higher standard and that's what I expect of myself and others. There is a strong emphasis on continuing education which I think is critical.

NAPFA has developed a very good questionnaire that you can use to interview financial advisors. We've reprinted it here with permission in Appendix B. It covers educational background, credentials, years of experience, the type of clients an advisor typically works with, fiduciary commitments, fee structure, the types of services offered and any problems with governing agencies. These are all very important questions to ask, but I have a few more suggestions I'd like to add.

My Criteria
After being in this business many years, here's what I think is important in choosing an advisor:

1. Heart
Find an advisor who cares about you. This is a trust business and you need to feel confident that your advisor knows who you are as a person and factors that into your planning.

2. Knowledge
It's not enough to be book smart. You have to work in this business at least five years before you really have a strong sense of what to do to help. It's also not enough to just be experienced. You need credentials that require continuing education. This business moves very quickly and keeping up is imperative. Hopefully experience plus credentials add up to wisdom.

3. Fiduciary Duty
A fiduciary is required to put your interests ahead of their own. It's important and you should insist on it.

4. Transparent Fees
You must know how your advisor is paid. My preference is for "fee only" advisors. We think that is the most transparent way of doing business.

5. Partnership and Continuity
You and your advisor are partners. Your advisor can only be effective if you are open and honest with each other. Don't be shy about fessing up if something has gone wrong. Remember, your advisor is on your side and is there to help. Also, look for an advisory practice that has advisors of varying ages. It takes a long time to jell as an organization, so it's important to bring on younger advisors early on. These younger professionals are an essential part of a thriving, lively practice that can live on past the original owner of the firm.

Fee-Only Advisors
I am an independent fee-only advisor and I always have been. That means my firm, Stevens Wealth Management, charges a transparent fee for our services and that's it. No commissions. No hidden fees. Very straight-forward. That's always been my preference because it just seems cleaner to me.

Critics of fee-only advisors will say that you pay a fee for services on top of brokerage fees for your investments. That's true. But if you keep your fee for service reasonable and the brokerage fees low, the costs can be reasonable and easy to understand.

NAPFA advisors are all fee-only advisors. You can find a NAPFA advisor near you at www.napfa.org. My friend Sheryl Garrett has founded a network of fee-only advisors that work on an hourly basis. You can read her book, *Just Give Me the Answer$*, or go to The Garrett Planning Network website at www.garrettplanningnetwork.com. Sheryl has authored many books including some in the *Dummies* series.

Finding That Trusted Advisor: Three Stories

Keep Interviewing Until It Clicks

When you're dating, they tell you that you may have to kiss a lot of frogs. When you're interviewing advisors, you may have to interview more than one to find the right fit. Here's one client's account of what they did:

> *"Prior to working with Stevens Wealth Management, my husband and I had never used an investment adviser. As the company I worked for went public and my partnership share moved to stock ownership, I knew time was not going to be on my side in climbing the learning curve of individual stocks, funds, and markets. The interviewing of investment advisers and managers began. The first was all high pressure. The second had a fee structure that negated the benefit of using him. The third wouldn't let me get a word in edgewise. And the fourth I simply didn't trust from the moment I met him.*
>
> *Sue was the fifth and I could tell as I walked through the door that this was going to be different. She asked questions, listened, reviewed the analysis I had brought, and answered each one of my long list of questions thoughtfully. She made some specific suggestions and recommendations based on the objectives we discussed (and I love specifics!) and made it clear there was no commitment to use her further – and no charge for the initial time we spent together as it was an opportunity to get to know each other and decide if the relationship was right for both of us. Needless to say, it was.*
>
> *The same low key, honest, open, and thoughtful approach has been present for many years now – through good markets and most recently through a poor one. It continues to be comforting to know that she's looking out for our best interest*

(including Sunday evening calls when things were degrading rapidly) and providing solid and well-considered counsel with clear decision points. It's allowed us to keep an eye on investments, but not be consumed by them, to have a partner in planning that enables us to achieve and adjust our objectives, and to always receive a straight-forward and easy to understand perspective. We're positioned well for retirement despite the market and still able to enjoy our life style with minor prudent modifications. In a market as volatile as 2008-2009, that's saying something!"

Finding the Right Fit

Building up trust with someone doesn't happen overnight. I encourage you to start the process early so that you find what you are looking for. Here's another client's story:

"About ten years ago, I started reading Sue's articles about finance. My husband was anticipating retiring and he had a substantial 401(k) plan that we planned to rollover to an IRA. We felt that we were both intelligent people and we could manage our finances – we had done fairly well. I always read Sue's articles and the more I read, the more I felt her investing philosophy matched our ideas. The bottom line is that the more we looked at the 'work' involved in managing finances, we knew that we did not want to spend our time doing that."

We've been working with Don and Marsha, the couple above, for eight years now. One of my favorite memories was when Don wanted to surprise Marsha with a very special trip. But she was the one who always watched the investment accounts carefully and he wasn't sure how to put down the deposit without tipping her off. We decided to open a small separate account where he could earmark the money for the trip. But sure enough, Marsha discovered the withdrawal and called me to see what was going on.

Now I had a dilemma. Don was very excited about surprising her and I didn't want to blow the surprise. And yet, I understood Marsha needed a straight-forward answer about her money. So I told her Don was planning something very special and she would need to talk to him. Then I quickly called him and filled him in.

Bottom line? Marsha was surprised and delighted by Don's thoughtfulness. They had a wonderful time and I believe this is a case of putting their money where their heart was.

Don and Marsha and I have lived through many years together financially. I've watched as Don has had a couple of very scary health concerns. We've talked about major charitable donations to not only worthwhile organizations, but individuals where the only motivation was kindness and love. No expectation of anything in return or even a tax deduction.

Don and Marsha live life as an adventure and I know they are happy. That doesn't mean life doesn't have its challenges—it has plenty. But they have each other and their family and their faith.

Finding Common Ground

If you think it's tricky to find the right balance of risk and reward for one person, try two. Most husbands and wives have separate opinions on most topics—what they like to eat, how they like to spend leisure time, what to watch on TV. Why should investing be any different? It's not uncommon for our firm to meet with new couples who just can't come to an agreement on what to do, especially in retirement.

Dieter and Jo came to us three years ago and had been married 42 years. They built a good life together and had retired in 1995. Jo found us through my writing and shared many articles with her husband. Over a two-year period they came to know my style and approach to money management.

> *"We had gone through some very turbulent down markets, in which our investments suffered more than we thought necessary. We had an investment advisor, but not a money manager. While that person had advised us well, his job was not to monitor our investments on an individual, daily basis.*
>
> *My husband and I had very different investing philosophies, and after the early 2000 down market, we more or less were in limbo. His investments were more aggressive and short-termed than mine, and thus we could not agree on any future investment plan.*

Finally, three years ago, my husband and I found one in-
vestment philosophy that we could agree on--we wanted and
needed someone to be our money manager so that our retire-
ment would be secure and enjoyable. Our current status was
no longer either!"

When I first met with Jo and Dieter, it was clear they were very concerned for two reasons: 1) the economy had taken a nose dive and so had
their portfolio and 2) as frequently happens, his risk tolerance was very
different from his wife's. We had a frank, open conversation about what really mattered to both of them. What everyone could agree on was that this
money they had accumulated was their nest egg and they wanted to stop
worrying that they would somehow "blow it" and face a future of worry
and scarcity.

When I manage portfolios, I usually look at all accounts in aggregate
and then divvy up the investments based on asset location (making the
best use of taxable and retirement accounts). I was able to design a portfolio that had elements of both growth and steady income that met Jo and
Dieter's goals. This is at the heart of Portfolio Peace of Mind™.

That's not to say that this cannot be achieved by the do-it-yourself investor. But in my experience, there are a lot of people that would just prefer
to leave this to someone else—providing they can find someone they trust.

"This last winter, we spent six weeks enjoying a winter re-
treat in Arizona, where we golfed, enjoyed friends, and most
of all, slept well while all the ugly financial news was blasting
us daily. We weathered the crisis with minimal losses; much
less than the average, and we are now positioned to take ad-
vantage of new investment avenues that should help us weath-
er whatever the future brings.

I can't tell you how much our decision has relieved our
financial and personal anxieties. It has given us time to enjoy
a disciplined lifestyle with ease and joy!"

Our Clients Hug Us and We Hug Back

....

"I just had my first hugging!" That was a comment from a new staff member in the last few months. Happily, most of our clients appreciate our work and they express it in many ways. In this case, one client had called another client the night before and asked if they thought it would be OK if they gave us a hug. The answer was "Yes" and it was a heartfelt gesture that was welcomed by us.

We feel genuine affection for our clients. We have a small practice and get to know our clients well. We want to help our clients reach their goals. We agonize when there are set-backs and try to bring all our expertise to bear to brainstorm how to get back on track as quickly as possible.

This is what you should expect from your advisor. There are people out there who love their work and are very good at it. Take the time to do a thorough interview process to find the right team to work with. In this electronic age, don't think it has to be someone in your local area unless you feel that you wouldn't be comfortable otherwise. We have clients all over the U.S. and I feel like I know them all very well even though in some cases we've never even met face-to-face.

Our Role As Advisors

Gandhi said "We must be the change we wish to see in the world." Our role as advisors is changing. It will demand challenging the status quo and looking at the future with fresh eyes. It will require that we not become complacent and that the best of our profession will voluntarily choose to ask "How can we help?"

Greatness is never a given. It must be earned. Our journey has never been one of shortcuts or settling for less. It has not been the path for the faint-hearted, for those who prefer leisure over work, or seek only the pleasure of riches and fame. Rather, it has been the risk-takers, the doers, the makers of things—some celebrated, but more often men and women obscure in their labor—who have carried us up the long, rugged path toward prosperity and freedom.
~ Barack Obama, Inaugural Address, January 20, 2009

Chapter Eight

Radiant Wealth™

Living A Life of Fulfillment

If the day and the night are such that you greet them with joy, and
life emits a fragrance like flowers and sweet-scented herbs, is more
elastic, more starry, more immortal –that is your success.
~ Thoreau, *Walden*

"Radiant Wealth™" is a state of mind. When you know you have everything you truly need and you can extend that sense of fulfillment to enrich the lives of others, you will find financial happiness. We invite you to put your money where your heart is and think beyond the traditional measures of wealth.

A Path Paved with Gold

We started this journey in Chapter One with "The Other Gold" and spent some time setting the stage with Ten Paths to Financial Happiness™. Success, for all of its outer trappings, ultimately comes from within. It radiates out.

Chapter Two, "The American Dream," gave you a foundation to create a plan to allocate your investible cash flow. It offered a contemporary view of how you can meet your hierarchy of needs at any level of wealth. You may want to start here to gain control of where your money goes as you build your assets. I've observed over the years that living within your means is a common trait of successful investors.

Throughout the book I've talked about the importance of balance. Chapter Three, "Where Is Your Money?," shows you not only how to create your personal balance sheet, but how to interpret what it's telling you. You've seen how you can transform negative liquidity into something far more valuable.

When most people think of money, they think of investing. In Chapter Four, "Portfolio Peace of Mind™," we examined the balancing act of risk and reward. I introduced a six-step comprehensive process including an extensive worksheet, *The Independent Portfolio Assessment*, to help you integrate all aspects of your personal financial situation. I also emphasized how congruency in your investment approach can align your values with your money.

You have the power to change your life—at any point along the journey. Chapter Five, "It's Not Just Retirement, It's the Rest of Your Life™" offers insight into primary considerations you'll need for that transformation. Before you take a leap of faith, you need to plan carefully paying attention to cash flow, withdrawal rates and health care needs.

Love is a common thread through all of these paths. Leaving a legacy and building a bridge for your survivors is at the heart of Chapter Six, "The Financial Bridge™." I gave you worksheets to inventory the location of important documents, detail who to contact, to provide for your pets' care and a checklist for your survivors. All of these exercises will challenge you to think about what you really want to happen in the future. That may provide the incentive you need to take action today.

My business is a trust business. That takes time to build for most people. Chapter Seven, "A Matter of Trust," gives you a detailed checklist (Appendix B) to use as you interview advisors, assuming you need one. Not everyone will. I also gave you my two cents worth about what really matters as you think about who to trust.

That leads us to this point, Chapter Eight. If we've been successful in this process, that "other gold" will start to radiate because you've not only been able to improve your own relationship with money, but because you have put yourself in a position to help others. That's "Radiant Wealth™." All the pieces of the puzzle working together in harmony and balance, congruent with your goals.

There is an alchemical relationship to this process. For those of you that aren't familiar with alchemy, it is the ancient art of turning lead into gold. Metaphorically in this case. Perhaps literally too.

Radiant Wealth™

We are committed to helping you continue your journey and have created a monthly e-newsletter entitled *Radiant Wealth*™. Our pledge to you is to bring you information and inspiration that will help you on your own financial journey. Each of us can make a difference little-by-little by educating ourselves on important topics and putting our money where our hearts are. In this way we can find financial happiness.

To us, achieving financial happiness means following your dreams—no matter what the size of your bank account or your budget. *Radiant Wealth*™ is all about using that illumination to improve not only your life, but the lives of others.

Each month we bring you articles with our latest thinking in four distinct departments:

The Focused Financial Vision™

The first step to an inspired financial life begins with understanding your relationship to money, what's going on in the world and setting your intention.

Portfolio Peace of Mind™

In the process of putting your money where your heart is, you need to educate yourself about financial issues and how they relate to meeting your objectives. By focusing on balance, you can find peace of mind.

It's Not Just Retirement, It's the Rest of Your Life™

Your intentions not only manifest in your own life, but in the world around you. The rest of your life is up to you. Learn about retirement-related issues including leaving a legacy.

Financial Feng Shui

Money is energy. You need to constantly re-focus and cleanse everything related to this energetic system so that it isn't stagnant and it supports a life you love.

We invite you to join our community of like-minded individuals who want to make the most of their financial resources to create "Radiant Wealth™." You can subscribe to *Radiant Wealth*™ at www.financial-happiness.com.

May the blessing of light be on you,
light without and light Within.
May the blessed sunshine shine on you
and warm your Heart till it glows
like a great peat fire, so that the stranger
may Come and warm himself at it,
and also a friend.
~ Traditional Irish Blessing

Stories of Radiant Wealth™

....

Megan's Story

Giving can take place in lots of different ways. Anyone can improve someone else's life, but if you've been blessed with significant wealth, there's even more opportunity to give.

Megan is someone I've known since she was ten years old. She studied the cello with me. She was always very bright and attended Yale University to study computers. She came from a modest Midwest family, as I did. My mom was her first grade teacher and she helped pay for Megan's cello lessons when she was young.

Megan and her husband Mike both worked for a major software development company for over ten years. Their company stock windfalls made them millionaires in their early thirties. That gave them the freedom to make major life changes. They both left the big jobs and the stress to try new ventures and to spend more time with their young family.

Megan and I talked about how she could use some of her own new-found wealth to help her parents. Here's her story:

> *"I think one of the things that I think about the most is how you've helped us set up an annuity for my parents. Although I was starting to have a bunch of money in my investment accounts, and I had a will to make sure my family would be taken care of if anything happened to me, I'd never thought about how to help my parents in a consistent way while I was still alive (and therefore while they were still alive). I was sending them money when I knew they needed it, and helping them with projects, but your suggestion of setting up the annuity made such a huge difference for me and for them. It allowed my mother to finally retire because she knew she could count on money from me (not just hope for it without being able to plan on it). It meant that no matter what happened to my finances, my financial ups and downs wouldn't have to impact my parents, they could still count on the annuity, even if I ended up having a tough year. And it removed the discomfort of trying to figure out if they had enough, or how*

much they needed, or whether my siblings were contributing right then, etc. It's peace of mind, really. For me and for them. I am very, very grateful to you for suggesting it, and helping to make it so easy for me to set up."

Annuities are not for everyone. We talked about one type of annuity—the fixed immediate annuity—in Chapter Five. In certain situations they can play a key role in providing ongoing security. Using your money to change someone else's life is clearly a good example of Radiant Wealth™. It goes beyond one life and affects many.

> *It is not how much we have,*
> *but how much we enjoy, that makes happiness.*
> ~ Charles Haddon Spurgeon

Barb's Story

Barb came to see us right after a painful divorce. She had spent her life in a wealthy North Shore suburb of Chicago and was very concerned about how she would survive going forward.

She was always very practical. We went to work using cash flow modeling software that helped project how much of her divorce proceeds (paid over an eight and one-half year period) she would need to save to have enough money over her lifetime. We talked about how much house she could afford and she actually chose something very modest. That was a very smart move. It has allowed her not to worry about cutting expenses too close.

She has a job at the park district and over the years she has done very well there. Her salary has increased and even more important, she has good benefits including health care. When we first started, she knew very little about personal finances. Says Barb:

> *"I think we were typical of many affluent couples where one partner has complete control over the finances and all decisions related to it. The partner who is not involved slowly stops asking questions and the division of power related to money is set in stone. It's easier not to know. It's easier not to worry. It isn't until you need to know that you realize just how*

*lost you are and how much control over your own future you
have given up."*

Boy has that changed. Barb has educated herself about the issues and
has taken time to help other women she works with who also need to learn
more. She talks to young women about the need to save. At a recent meeting with us she happily announced that these young women (all in their
20s) have all made great progress on setting up their emergency fund reserves. Some have also opened their first investment accounts, either Roth
IRAs or mutual fund accounts.

> *"Many, many wealthy women, even those in good, healthy
> marriages have no idea how dependent upon their husbands
> they really are and they won't know unless something hap-
> pens. I have come a long way since the day we met and you
> handed me a big box of Kleenex."*

A few years back, Barb and I talked about her dream for the future. We
both love farms and she shared that she'd love to have a little farm where
she could raise a couple goats. I shared that I had a farm in Pennsylvania
(when I worked for The Vanguard Group) and the barn was called "The
Lofty Goat." The people I bought the 200-year old barn from had raised
goats.

After the awful stock market routing we had in the past couple years,
Barb made a comment to a co-worker that perhaps the dream of the goat
farm was gone. The co-worker told her to give us a call to help reassure her
if we were still on track or not. And she gave Barb a picture of a smiling
goat that she could look at when she was feeling down.

Barb came in for a meeting (and she's going to be just fine!) and
brought us a present—a picture of that same smiling goat. It is now proudly
displayed in our office. And we're talking about how we might be able to
partner on some seminars to help educate more women through her park
district program.

Those dreams of your heart are what I'm talking about when I say
put your money where your heart is. They keep you going even when times
are tough.

Charitable Giving

The best way to find yourself is to lose
yourself in the service to others.
~ Gandhi

One of the universal paradoxes is that if you want to start feeling better yourself, do something for someone else. It's human nature to want to reach out a helping hand. That includes how you allocate your assets.

There are so many ways to spread the wealth. There are worthwhile charities that help people in need, animals, the environment, the arts, education—you name it. As we discussed in Chapter Two, we all have a hierarchy of needs that includes developing our own self-esteem and self-actualization as well as helping others. The final stage of Maslow's model was transcendence—going beyond ourselves.

Giving to organizations that live on after your life is over creates a legacy. Find an organization that speaks to you in a way that invites you to share in supporting someone or something that you really love. That's a major part of Putting Your Money Where Your Heart Is.

Besides being something that makes you feel good, charitable giving is also a smart financial move. You can take a tax deduction for most of your donations. You can also name charities in your estate documents that may decrease the amount of tax owed at your death.

Put Your Money Where Your Heart Is™

. . . .

This phrase has multiple levels of meaning. Take it for whatever it means to you. It can mean investing in securities that represent what you hold in high esteem for the future. It can mean creating a spending plan that gives you the freedom to follow your passion. Perhaps you can find a way to light up a path for millions of others. Or just one other. Any of these things would make me happy.

"This is where inner and outer happiness seem to converge. And, come to think of it, this principle isn't limited only to particular positive mental states like hope, optimism, or trust, but in fact it seems that all of the positive emotions and happiness in general, all share this same quality, the potential of promoting both inner and outer happiness. It reminds me of all the studies showing how happy individuals are more altruistic, more willing to reach out and help, more charitable—so here again, inner happiness and working toward a better world seem to merge. And, it works the other way too. Not only is it the case that happy people are more willing to help others, but as I generally mention, helping others is the best way to help yourself, the best way to promote your own happiness. It is you, yourself, who will receive the benefit.

~His Holiness The Dalai Lama and Howard C. Cutler, MD,
The Art of Happiness in a Troubled World

Appendix A – The Independent Portfolio Assessment

The Independent Portfolio Assessment

Your Name	*Age:*
Your Spouse's Name	*Age:*
Your Children's Names	*Age:*
Your Parent's Names	*Age:*

What Matters Most (Where Your Heart Is)

Long-Term Objectives as of:

Next Year's Objectives

Net Worth Statement

Net Worth (Inception)	*Date:*
Net Worth (Current)	*Date:*

- ✓ Is the level of emergency reserves adequate?
- ✓ Is the level of debt reasonable?
- ✓ Look at debt/income ratio
- ✓ Can you restructure the debt?
- ✓ Is there balance?

Credit

Credit Report Reviewed	*Date:*

The Independent Portfolio Assessment   *(continued)*

Portfolio Details
Current Date:

Asset Class	Current Allocation	IPS	Revised IPS
Cash			
Domestic Fixed Income*			
Intl Fixed Income			
Large-Cap Stock*			
Mid-Small-Cap Stock			
Intl Stock			
Alternative			
Other			

*Balanced funds are split 50/50 between fixed income and large-cap stocks

Portfolio Specifics	Data
Total Return Prior Year:	%
Total Return Most Recent Quarter:	%
Total Return Since Inception:	%
Inception Date:	
Risk Tolerance:	
Expected Range of Returns:	%
Current Liquidity Reserve :	$
Last Rebalance Date:	

Tax Return   *Date:*

Adjusted Gross Income (p.1):	
Taxable Income (p.2):	
Year-to-Date Realized Gains/Losses:	
Loss Carry-forwards (Schedule D):	
Marginal Tax Rate:	

✓ Is the portfolio tax-efficient?
✓ Review asset location

The Independent Portfolio Assessment   *(continued)*

Retirement Plan

Projected Retirement Date

Current Expenses

Projected Expenses at Retirement

On Track?

Retirement Considerations

✓ Any IRA contributions for current year/any catch-up contributions?

✓ Maxing out on company retirement contributions? Match?

✓ Any required minimum distributions from retirement accounts?

✓ Consider conversion to Roth IRA?

✓ Upcoming changes within personal/company retirement plans?

✓ Estimated rate of withdrawal: __%

✓ Long-term care insurance? Carrier?

Education Funding

Child's Name, Age:

Years Until College:

Type of Funding Vehicle:

Balance:

Contributions:

Date of Last Analysis:

Change Allocation? (yes/no)

Date of Last Change:

Estate Planning

✓ Do you have documents?

✓ Do you need to update your documents?

✓ Are your trusts funded?

✓ Check beneficiary designations for investment accounts, life insurance policies, retirement plans

✓ Gifting strategies?

Appendix B – Napfa Financial Planner Diagnostic

Comprehensive Financial
Advisor Diagnostic

How do you sift through the hype when looking for a comprehensive financial advisor? Will a firm with a huge advertising budget do the best job helping you meet life's financial goals? TV ads may talk about your hopes and dreams, but ultimately salespeople focus almost exclusively on selling investment products and insurance. Your financial situation is complex; a truly comprehensive financial advisor will analyze your current condition, make prudent recommendations and support you along the way.

The *Comprehensive Financial Advisor Diagnostic*, created by the National Association of Personal Financial Advisors (NAPFA) is a thorough questionnaire you can use to evaluate a financial advisor. The questions and popular *answer key* will help you make an informed decision based on the responses a financial advisor provides. Before hiring a financial planning professional, perform this simple diagnostic. If the advisor's answers do not follow prudent core values, you may not be engaging the right advisor for you.

1. What is your educational background?
    College Degree: ☐ Yes ☐ No   Area of Study: _____
    Graduate Degree: ☐ Yes ☐ No   Area of Study: _____

2. What are your financial planning credentials/designations and affiliations? (Check all that apply)
    NAPFA-Registered Financial Advisor ☐
    Certified Financial Planner (CFP) ☐
    Chartered Financial Consultant (ChFC) ☐
    Certified Public Accountant/Personal Financial Specialist (CPA/PFS) ☐
    Master of Science, Financial Services (MSFS) ☐
    Financial Planning Association (FPA) ☐
    Other: _____

3. How long have you been offering financial planning services?
    ☐ Less than 2 years   ☐ 2-5 years   ☐ 5-10 years   ☐ More than 10 years

4. Will you provide me with references from other professionals?
    ☐ Yes   ☐ No
    (If no, please explain)_____

5. Have you ever been cited by a professional or regulatory governing body for disciplinary reasons?
    ☐ Yes   ☐ No
    (If yes, please explain) _____

6. How many clients do you work with?_____

7. Are you currently engaged in any other business, either as a sole proprietor, partner, officer, employee, trustee, agent or otherwise? (Exclude non-investment related activities which are exclusively charitable, civic, religious or fraternal and are recognized as tax-exempt.)
    ☐ Yes   ☐ No
    (If yes, please explain)_____

8. Will you or an associate work with me?
    I will ☐   An associate will ☐   Act as a Team ☐
    (If an associate will be my primary contact, complete questions 1-8 for each associate as well.)

Fee ⬤ Only

Comprehensive Financial
Advisor Diagnostic

9.   Will you sign the Fiduciary Oath below?
☐   Yes   ☐   No

<u>Fiduciary Oath</u>
The advisor shall exercise his/her best efforts to act in good faith and in the best interests of the client. The advisor shall provide written disclosure to the client prior to the engagement of the advisor, and thereafter throughout the term of the engagement, of any conflicts of interest, which will or reasonably may compromise the impartiality or independence of the advisor.

The advisor, or any party in which the advisor has a financial interest, does not receive any compensation or other remuneration that is contingent on any client's purchase or sale of a financial product. The advisor does not receive a fee or other compensation from another party based on the referral of a client or the client's business.

Following the NAPFA Fiduciary Oath means I shall:

* *Always act in good faith and with candor*
* *Be proactive in disclosing any conflicts of interest that may impact a client*
* *Not accept any referral fees or compensation contingent upon the purchase or sale of a financial product*

_____

Signature

10.   Do you have a business continuity plan?
☐   Yes   ☐   No
(If no, please explain)_____

Compensation

Financial planning costs include what a client pays in fees and commissions. Comparison between advisors requires full information about potential total costs. It is important to have this information before entering into any agreement.

11.   How is your firm compensated and how is your compensation calculated?
☐   Fee-Only (as calculated below):
        Hourly rate of $ _____/hour
        Flat fee (Range and Explanation) _____
        Percentage _____% to _____% of _____
                 (AUM, Net worth, etc.)
☐   Commissions only; from securities, insurance, and/or other products that clients buy from a firm with which you are associated.
☐   Fee and Commissions (fee-based)
☐   Fee Offset, (charging a flat fee against which commissions are offset.) If the commissions exceed the fee, is the balance credited to me? ☐ Yes ☐ No

Fee **FO** Only
™

12. Do you have an agreement describing your compensation and services that will be provided in advance of the engagement?

☐ Yes   ☐ No

13. Do you have a minimum fee?

☐ Yes   ☐ No

(If yes, please explain) _____

14. If you earn commissions, approximately what percentage of your firm's commission income comes from:

_____% Insurance products   _____% Stocks and bonds
_____% Annuities   _____% Coins, tangibles, collectibles
_____% Mutual Funds   _____% Limited Partnerships
_____% Other:_____

15. Does any member of your firm act as a general partner, participate in, or receive compensation from investments you may recommend to me?

☐ Yes   ☐ No

16. Do you receive referral fees from attorneys, accountants, insurance agents, mortgage brokers, or others?

☐ Yes   ☐ No

17. Do you receive on-going income from any of the mutual funds that you recommend in the form of "12(b)1" fees, "trailing" commissions, or other continuing payouts?

☐ Yes   ☐ No

18. Are there financial incentives for you to recommend certain financial products?

☐ Yes   ☐ No

(If yes, please explain) _____

Services

Financial planners provide a range of services. It is important to match your needs with services provided.

19. Do you offer advice on? (check all that apply)

Goal setting ☐   Estate planning ☐
Cash management & budgeting ☐   Insurance needs ☐
Tax planning ☐   Education funding ☐
Investment review & planning ☐   Retirement planning ☐
Other:_____

20. Do you provide a comprehensive written analysis of my financial situation and recommendations?

☐ Yes   ☐ No

Fee Only™

Comprehensive Financial
Advisor Diagnostic

21. Do you offer assistance with implementation with the plan?
     ☐   Yes   ☐   No

22. Do you offer continuous, on-going advice regarding my financial affairs, including advice on non-investment related financial issues?
     ☐   Yes   ☐   No

23. Other than receiving my permission to debit my investment account for your fee, do you take custody of, or will you have access to, my assets?
     ☐   Yes   ☐   No

24. If you were to provide me on-going investment advisory services, do you require "discretionary" trading authority over my investment accounts?
     ☐   Yes   ☐   No

Regulatory Compliance

Federal and state laws require that, under most circumstances, individuals or firms holding themselves out to the public as providing investment advisory services are required to be registered with either the U. S. Securities & Exchange Commission (SEC) or the regulatory agency of the state in which the individual/firm conducts business.

25. I am (or my firm) is registered as an Investment Advisor?
     ☐   Yes   (In the State of   )☐   No

Please provide your Form ADV Part II or brochure being used in compliance with the Investment Advisors Act of 1940. If not registered with either the SEC or any state, please indicate the specific reason (regulatory exemption or other reason) for non-registration.

Signature of Advisor:_____   Firm Name:_____

Date:_____

Please Note:
A yes or no answer requiring explanation is not necessarily a cause for concern. We encourage you to give the advisor an opportunity to explain any response. Information geared to the investing public can be found on the Securities & Exchange Commission website (www.sec.gov) under the "Investor Information" section.

This form was created by the National Association of Personal Financial Advisors (NAPFA) to assist consumers in selecting a personal financial advisor. It can be used as a checklist during an interview, or sent to prospective advisors as a part of a preliminary screening. NAPFA recommends that individuals from at least two different firms be interviewed.

Comprehensive Financial
Advisor Diagnostic

Answer Key

Once you have a completed *Diagnostic* in hand it's time to evaluate the responses. NAPFA provides the following Answer Key based on the long-standing ideals of the organization:

Question #1 – Although not currently required by applicable regulatory authorities, NAPFA believes that a financial advisor should have an advanced education in financial planning topics such as investments, taxes, insurance, or estate planning in addition to a college degree. Also, NAPFA believes that your planner should be required to participate in continuing professional education to keep his/her knowledge base current.

Question #2 – There are a number of professional certifications or designations financial advisors can obtain, and each requires a different level of Continuing Education requirements to maintain. It is important to take the Continuing Education requirements into account when selecting an advisor, since one may assume the more Continuing Education required by the governing body she/he belongs to, the more knowledgeable the advisor. Continuing Education also helps advisors stay on top of trends in the industry, which should help them make better recommendations for your financial situation.

- NAPFA-Registered Financial Advisor — = 60 hrs every 2 years
- Certified Financial Planner (CFP) — = 30 hrs every 2 years
- Chartered Financial Consultant (ChFC) — = 30 hrs every 2 years
- Certified Public Accountant/Personal Financial Specialist (CPA/PFS) — = 60** hrs every 3 years (min.)
- Financial Planning Association Member — = No CE required

** Requirement ranges between 60 and 135 hours every three years based on total hours of business experience.

Question #3 – Just because someone has one of the above listed designations does not by itself mean that person is a truly competent financial advisor. You should carefully examine a person's background and experience when choosing an advisor; someone who has been in the industry longer and provides comprehensive financial planning may be a better fit for you, especially if you have a complicated financial situation.

Question #4 – If you request, the financial advisor filling out the Diagnostic should also be willing to share the name of another financial professional with whom he/she has worked. By talking with another financial professional who is familiar with the prospective financial advisor you might be better able to learn more about their abilities and strategies for recommending prudent courses of action. Privacy laws severely limit an advisor's ability to share client information.

Question #5 – Be wary of a financial advisor who has been disciplined by a professional or regulatory body. In many cases, financial advisors who are disciplined are being held accountable for imprudent advice or abuse. You should, however, give an advisor the opportunity to explain his/her side of the disciplinary incident.

Question #6 – Personal attention is important when engaging a financial advisor. The number of clients an advisor works with will help you better understand how much attention she/he will be able to devote to you and your situation. If the number of clients seems excessive, ask how advising that many clients will affect your relationship.

Question #7 – By knowing what other business ventures a financial advisor is involved in, you will better understand if there are any conflicts of interest with regard to the advice that you might receive. This is especially important if the advisor is involved with any other investment related entity. If there is a relationship in place with another conflicting organization, ask for a detailed account of how that relationship will impact the advice she/he will provide you.

Question #8 – When engaging a financial advisor, you will want to know whether you will be working with that person directly or another qualified professional who is part of a team. If the advisor indicates that an associate will primarily work with you, ask to meet that person prior to commencing the relationship.

Question #9 – Accountability is important in financial planning. While there are many people in the financial services industry who profess to have the client's best interests at heart, they still may make recommendations that present a conflict of interest. NAPFA requires all of its members to sign a Fiduciary Oath; this helps to ensure that each client's best interests, not the advisor's, are always a priority.

Question #10 – A concern for many clients is they will retain the services of a financial advisor who might soon retire, pass away, or transition completely out of financial services. If any of these events were to occur, what would happen to you? You should ask your prospective financial advisor if she/he has a plan in place to address any potential situations whereby she/he might no longer be able to provide services. .

Question #11 – How should a financial advisor charge for services? The members of NAPFA firmly believe that financial advisors should charge Fee-Only. Although NAPFA recognizes that financial planners can provide services on a commission basis, it is NAPFA's core position that a Fee-Only engagement removes the potential conflicts of interest that are inherent in a commission relationship.

Question #12 – Prior to formalizing a relationship, a financial advisor should always provide you information which clearly discloses how she/he will be compensated: Fee-Only, commissions, etc. Ask for this information prior to commencing a relationship, and if there are any corresponding conflicts of interest presented by the compensation arrangement.

Question #13 – Financial advisors may charge a minimum fee for services they render. If you have limited financial planning needs and/or a small portfolio, paying a minimum fee may not be in your best interests. If that is your situation, search for an advisor who will provide you professional advice on a flat-fee, project, or hourly basis.

Question #14 – While NAPFA encourages you to consider using a Fee-Only Financial Advisor to minimize the potential for conflicts of interest, you may instead select an advisor who accepts commissions. Financial advisors who are compensated based on commissions should be able to explain how they are compensated and identify what percentage of their compensation is derived from the sale of various commission-based investment products and/or securities trading.

Question #15 – Ask your prospective financial advisor if she/he is limited to presenting certain types of investments or investment products to you. If so, inquire why she/he is limited, and how this might impact the success of attaining your goals and/or the amount of fees to be paid.

Question #16 – As you work with a financial advisor, other needs revolving around important financial issues will become evident. Certain advisors, for example, recommend attorneys, accountants, insurance agents, and mortgage brokers to their clients. You should inquire whether the financial advisor will receive a referral fee from the recommended professional. If the financial advisor does receive a referral fee or some other type of compensation from the professional(s) that she/he may recommend to you, you should seriously consider this conflict of interest prior to engaging the recommended professional.

Question #17 – Some mutual fund and investment product sponsors pay 12b(1) and similar fees. A financial advisor who receives 12(b)1 fees or "trailers" is not a Fee-Only Financial Advisor. Trailing fees may negatively impact you, because typically the product sponsor charges shareholders higher fees and then pays a portion of the money to the financial advisor on an ongoing basis.

Comprehensive Financial
Advisor Diagnostic

Question #18 – Commission-based advisors may receive higher commissions on certain products they sell than on others. This may influence their decision to recommend investment products that are not in your best interest. Ask your prospective financial advisor how his/her recommendation might impact the success of attaining your goals and/or the amount of fees to be paid. Fee-Only advisors do not have this conflict of interest; they are able to recommend investments based solely upon your specific needs.

Question #19 – Many financial professionals loosely use the term "Comprehensive" in describing their range of financial planning services. Financial planning is generally much more than simply developing a plan for primarily short-term objectives and reviewing the plan when appropriate. Comprehensive financial planning typically covers a wide range of both short- and long-term financial issues and addresses your personal goals, objectives and significant life cycle events. The more services your financial advisor provides, the greater your odds of receiving truly comprehensive financial planning.

Question #20 – The financial advisor that you engage should be willing and able to provide you with a written analysis of your current financial situation as well as appropriate corresponding recommendations to help you accomplish your objectives. This written analysis can serve as the starting point for beginning your client/advisor relationship.

Question #21 – The development of a comprehensive financial plan is the initial step to properly assessing your finances. A plan, however, has little value until it is implemented. As opposed to 'going it alone', consider having your financial advisor implement the plan. Fee-Only advisors can often reduce your investment costs by investing in assets with reduced annual expenses and no related sales commissions.

Question #22 – Some consumers find regular or periodic reviews and on-going communication necessary to remain on track toward achieving financial objectives. If this level of involvement is important to you, make sure the financial advisor you hire provides this ongoing support.

Question #23 – While allowing an advisor to debit your investment account for her/his fee is fairly typical, you should avoid permitting an advisor to have physical "custody of your investment assets", or the ability to make withdrawals or transfers from your account(s) without express specific prior written consent prior to each such withdrawal or transfer. Generally, Fee-Only advisors will not expose their clients to these "custody" type situations. When you use a Fee-Only advisor, an unaffiliated brokerage firm will usually maintain physical custody of your investment assets.

Question #24 – If you grant an advisor "discretionary" trading authority over your investment account, the advisor can place orders to either buy or sell securities without consulting with you ahead of time. If you have granted your advisor "non-discretionary" trading authority, the advisor must obtain your approval prior to making any transactions in your account. If you are going to grant "discretionary" authority to your advisor, prior to making the initial investments, it is advisable to have a written document setting forth the terms and conditions of the discretionary engagement (usually set forth in an Investment Management Agreement). Additionally you should receive a corresponding written document setting forth the investment parameters for the accounts to be managed (i.e. investment objectives, percentage allocations, restrictions, etc), often referred to as an Investment Policy Statement. Of course, you should always continue to monitor the activity within your investment account to make sure that transactions are within the parameters of an agreed-upon investment policy.

Question #25 – NAPFA believes that any financial advisor offering comprehensive financial planning services should be registered as an investment advisor with either the U.S. Securities and Exchange Commission (SEC) or with the state regulatory agency within the advisor's state. Information pertaining to both SEC registered investment advisors (and the vast majority of state registered investment advisors) is set forth on Part I of the advisor's Form ADV (see www.sec.gov). Unlike other investment professionals, only registered investment advisors owe a fiduciary duty under law to their clients (i.e. they are required to always act in the best interests of their clients and to make full and fair disclosure of all material facts, especially when the adviser's interests may conflict with those of the client).

Appendix C – Recommended Reading

Lighting the Torch, George Kinder (FPA Press, 2006)

It's Not About the Money, Brett Kessel (HarperOne, 2008)

The Four Pillars of Investing, William Bernstein (McGraw-Hill, 2002)

Asset Allocation, Roger C. Gibson (McGraw-Hill, 2000)

The Little Book of Common Sense Investing, John C. Bogle (Wiley, 2007)

Enough, John C. Bogle (Wiley, 2009)

Morningstar Guide to Mutual Funds, Christine Benz (Wiley, 2005)

The ETF Book, Rick Ferri (Wiley, 2008)

The Wealthy Barber, David Chilton (Prima, 1991)

The Post-American World, Fareed Zakaria (Norton, 2008)

Your Money & Your Brain, Jason Zweig (Simon & Schuster, 2008)

Your Complete Retirement Planning Road Map, Ed Slott (Ballantine, 2007)

A Commonsense Guide to Your 401(k), Mary Rowland (Bloomberg, 1998)

Life and Death Planning for Retirement Benefits,
Natalie Choate (Ataxplan, 2006)

Retirement Income Redesigned, edited by Harold Evensky
and Deena B. Katz (Bloomberg, 2006)

Conserving Client Portfolios During Retirement, William P. Bengen (FPA
Press, 2006)

Saving for Retirement, Gail Marks Jarvis (FT Press, 2007)

How to Retire Happy, Wild, and Free, Ernie J. Zelinski
(Ten Speed Press, 2004)

Long-Term Care, Phyllis Shelton (Kensington, 2001)

Just Give Me the Answer$, Sheryl Garrett (Kaplan, 2004)

Glossary

....

401(k) plan – An employer-sponsored retirement plan that permits participants to make pre-tax contributions, and may include an employer matching contribution. (Many plans also allow participants to make after-tax contributions.) 401(k) plans are considered "tax-advantaged" plans because pre-tax contributions lower the employee's taxable income, and taxes are due on earnings only once the money is withdrawn from the plan. In most cases, withdrawals from the plan prior to age 59 ½ are subject to a 10% penalty.

403(b) plan – An employer-sponsored retirement plan most typically used by non-profit or not-for-profit organizations, such as colleges, hospitals, and schools. Like better-known 401(k) plans, most 403(b) plans permit participants to make pre- or after-tax contributions and include an employer matching contribution. Also, like 401(k) plans, 403(b) plans are considered "tax-advantaged" plans because pre-tax contributions lower the employee's taxable income, and taxes are due on earnings only once the money is withdrawn from the plan. In most cases, withdrawals from the plan prior to age 59 ½ are subject to a 10% penalty.

457 plan – An employer-sponsored retirement plan used by primarily government employees. Like a 401(k), it allows participants to make pre-tax contributions, and defers any taxes due on investment gains. It differs from 401(k) plans primarily in that withdrawals prior to age 59 ½ are not subject to a 10% penalty.

Alternative investments – Traditionally defined as investments other than stocks, bonds, or cash, and can include real estate, precious metals, commodities, etc.

Annuity – A tax-deferred financial instrument in which the investor places money today (or over a period of time) and in return, receives a stream of payments in the future during the annuitization period. There are multitudes of ways in which annuities can be constructed, but in essence, the purchaser of an annuity is exchanging a fixed sum in the present for an income stream in the future.

Bond – A type of investment security, bonds are essentially loans. Typically, governments or large corporations issue bonds. Investors purchase these bonds, and in return receive a fixed amount of interest for the bond's term (which can be as short as a few months or as long as 30 years). At the end of the term, the bond holder receives their original investment back. Most bonds are priced daily, and can be bought and sold on the open market.

Bond mutual fund – A mutual fund that invests in bonds. This is a broad classification, and includes many sub-categories, including bond funds that invest only in tax-exempt bonds, Treasury bonds, or corporate bonds, and funds that invest only in short-, intermediate-, or long-term bonds.

Capital contributions – Cash or property given by a shareholder or owner to a corporation. In exchange for the capital contribution, the shareholder or owner receives an increase in the basis of their existing stock or some other type of ownership interest.

Capital gains tax – A tax on investment gains or losses. A complex system of netting gains and losses is allowed each year. Current rates are either 10% or 15% of the net gain (in most cases).

Cash poor – When you hold little or no cash and your assets are tied up in things that can't be liquidated easily.

Certificate of Deposit (CD) – A savings instrument most often purchased from a bank or credit union. They're similar to savings deposits in that they're insured and free from market risk (i.e. changes in value). They differ in that they have a fixed maturity, which typically ranges from three months to five years. During this period, CDs pay interest at a rate that is usually fixed. If sold before maturity, the holder may be required to forfeit some of the interest they've earned.

Collectibles – Any assets such as antiques, art work, musical instruments, stamps, coins, etc.

Company stock – See Employer stock.

Credit Union – A financial institution, much like a bank, that is owned by its members.

Debt-to-income ratio – Allows you to see how much of your cash flow is going toward paying off debt obligations. Divide debt by income. Our recommendation is to play it safe and not exceed 22% for home-related debt and 30% for all debt.

Defined benefit (DB) plan – Most commonly refers to a type of pension plan in which the employee is eligible for a fixed benefit upon retirement. The amount the employee is eligible for is typically subject to a vesting schedule, in which their benefit amount increases with their years of service.

Defined contribution (DC) plan – Retirement plans in which the amount invested is fixed, but the retirement benefit is dependent upon investment performance. Most DC plans are funded by employee contributions only. Some are funded by a combination of employer and employee contributions.

Emergency reserves – Savings set aside to cover a period of living expenses in the event of an emergency such as a period of unemployment. Typically invested in a liquid vehicle such as a money market account, emergency reserves should cover a minimum of three months' worth of expenses. An emergency fund can prevent the investor from having to tap into more volatile assets—such as stock or bond funds—to fund living expenses.

Employer stock – Stock owned by an employee of the firm that employs them. It is most typically accumulated by way of an Employer Stock Purchase Plan, a Stock Option Plan, or a Restricted Stock Plan.

Estate tax – The tax the government levies on your assets after you die. If your estate is under $3.5 million (2009), you won't owe federal estate tax.

Exchange-traded funds (ETFs) – An investment vehicle that is structured much like an index mutual fund, an ETF owns a group of stocks or bonds and is designed to track a specific index. Some ETFs track broad indexes, like the S&P 500, and some track small sectors, like energy stocks. Unlike mutual funds, ETFs can be bought and sold throughout the day.

Exercise price – The price at which stock options can be exercised and used to purchase actual shares of stock.

Fixed annuity – A tax-deferred savings instrument in which the beneficiary makes an initial contribution today (or over a period of time) and receives an income stream in the future (typically covering the beneficiary's lifetime). A fixed annuity pays a predetermined amount of income each period. This amount generally does not vary from year to year.

Fixed income – Bonds issued by entities either based in the United States (domestic) or outside of the U.S. (foreign).

Gross estate – The value of all of your assets after you die, before deductions and taxes.

Home equity line of credit – Similar to a home equity loan, a home equity line of credit allows you to tap into any equity you have in your home. Unlike a home equity loan, a line of credit merely approves you to tap a given amount in the future, much like a credit card allows you to charge up to a certain amount in the future.

Incentive stock options – A type of employee stock option. They offer a tax benefit in that the owner of the stock option does not have to pay ordinary income tax at exercise on the difference between the exercise price and the stock's market price if the shares are held for one year from the date of exercise and two years from the date they were granted. If these criteria are met, any gain made on the eventual sale of the shares would be taxed as a long-term capital gain.

Individual retirement account (IRA) – A savings vehicle that provides tax benefits, and is designed to accumulate savings to be used in retirement. The tax benefits vary by IRA type. The IRS has strict eligibility requirements that must be met in order to invest in an IRA. See also Traditional IRA, Roth IRA, Inherited IRA, and Rollover IRA.

Individual stock – A type of investment security that grants partial ownership of a corporation. Issued in shares, stocks are priced and actively traded throughout the day.

Inherited IRA – An IRA that is left to a beneficiary after the original owner's death. A spouse who inherits an IRA can roll it into his or her own existing IRA; non-spousal beneficiaries must keep the inherited IRA separate from their own accounts.

International stock – Stock issued by non-U.S. corporations.

Investment policy statement – A document that captures your objectives for investing and sets up the parameters for monitoring.

Large-cap stock – Stock issued by large, blue chip corporations. The 500 firms that comprise the S&P 500 index are typical examples.

Leverage – Borrowing against your current assets.

Liabilities – Amounts that are owed to outside entities, such as loans, mortgages, credit card balances, and any lines of credit that have been tapped.

Liquid assets – Assets that are readily exchanged into cash (such as checking accounts, savings accounts, and money market accounts).

Lump sum distribution – Refers to a withdrawal from a retirement account (401(k), IRA, or pension plan) in which the entire balance is taken out at once, as opposed to taking smaller distributions over a period of time.

Marketable – An asset that is easily sold. Stocks and mutual funds are marketable, in that it is very easy to find a buyer. Art or real estate, by comparison, are not considered marketable investments because it often takes longer to find a buyer for these assets.

Mid/Small-cap stock – Stock issued by smaller corporations, typically defined as those with a market capitalization below $10 billion.

Money market – A type of short-term savings account. Many money markets offered by banks, Savings and Loans, and credit unions are covered under FDIC insurance, while those offered by mutual fund firms are not. Money markets typically offer a slightly higher yield than savings accounts.

Municipal bonds – A bond with interest payments that are exempt from federal, and, in some cases, state taxes. They're typically issued by state and local governments.

Mutual funds – A type of investment in which assets of many investors are pooled together and managed by an investment professional. With total assets of over $12 trillion, mutual funds are the most common way that individuals invest in stocks and bonds. There are many types of mutual funds, but the broadest classifications are those that invest exclusively in stocks, those that invest only in bonds, and those that invest in a mix of stocks and bonds (which are known as balanced funds).

Negative liquidity – When you owe more than you own in liquid assets.

Net worth – Your personal balance sheet showing what you own minus what you owe.

Non-qualified stock options – Stock options that do not receive the beneficial tax treatment that incentive stock options do. Ordinary income tax is due on the difference between the fair market value of the stock and the exercise price at the time of exercise.

Non-vested – Can refer to stock options or retirement account balances. It is the balance that you would forfeit if you left your employer today. Employees typically become vested over a period of time, meaning that a larger portion of the employer's contribution to their retirement or stock option plan legally belongs to them.

Ordinary income tax – Federal tax levied on earned income or retirement account distributions as opposed to capital gains tax that is levied on the growth of assets held in taxable accounts.

Outstanding loans – Refers to any loans taken from a retirement account that have not yet been fully paid back. Typically a feature offered in 401(k) plans, any outstanding loans not paid back when employment terminates are subject to income taxes and, possibly, a 10% early withdrawal penalty.

Ownership interest – That portion of an asset that you legally own.

Pension plan – A type of retirement account which is funded by employer contributions. Those assets are then invested and managed on the employees' behalf. Upon retirement, the employee is eligible to receive a retirement benefit. Some pension plans allow the employee to take a lump-sum distribution upon retirement, and others only allow the employee to receive a benefit paid over their (and, if applicable, their spouse's) lifetimes.

Pre-tax balance – The balance of an investment account before any taxes owed are deducted.

Receivable – Money that is legally owed to you. Only include any amounts on your Net Worth Statement that you realistically expect to collect.

Restricted stock – Typically used as a form of compensation, in which the beneficiary is granted a given number of shares that are initially restricted from sale. There are a variety of conditions under which the beneficiary becomes vested in the stock, including things like time on the job and the achievement of corporate financial targets.

Rollover IRA – An IRA that consists of money that has been transferred directly from an employer-sponsored retirement plan, such as a 401(k).

Roth IRA – An IRA that does not permit the owner to deduct contributions from their federal income tax. In exchange for forgoing this benefit, the owner is allowed to withdraw their assets at retirement free of any federal tax on its earnings, as long as the account is at least five years old, and the beneficiary is at least 59 ½ years old. Also, unlike a Traditional IRA, contributions to a Roth IRA can be withdrawn at any time free of taxes or penalties. No minimum required distributions are necessary at age 70$1/2$.

Savings bond – A non-marketable security (meaning that it's not able to be sold to another investor) issued by the U.S. Treasury. There are two types of savings bonds. Series EE bonds earn a fixed rate of interest for periods of up to 30 years. I Savings Bonds pay an interest rate that is composed of two parts: a fixed rate, and an inflation rate. I-bonds are guaranteed to provide a rate of return above inflation.

Stable Value – A fixed income type of investment that invests in short-term insurance contracts. It's somewhat of a cross between cash and bonds.

Standard deviation – A statistical measure of volatility that depicts how widely dispersed a series of numbers is from the group's average. In a normally distributed population (the height of adult males, for example), 95 percent of all members of the group will fall within two standard deviations of the group's average.

Stock mutual fund – A mutual fund that invests only in stocks. Stock funds can follow a wide variety of strategies, including those that focus on international stocks, small company stocks, and funds that focus on a particular sector of the market. Actively managed stock funds are run by a manager who tries to earn the highest return possible. Index stock funds simply own a representative mix of all of the stocks in a given market index, like the S&P 500, and don't attempt to earn a return above that of the index.

Stock options – Typically offered as a form of compensation, stock options allow the beneficiary to purchase shares of the employer's stock at a given price (known as the exercise price) that is (hopefully) below the price that the shares are trading at on the open market.

Tax diversification – A strategy that attempts to protect the investor from future changes in tax rates and policy. Typically, it entails owning a variety of assets that are taxed differently (such as stocks, bonds, real estate, etc.) and making use of accounts that are taxed differently (such as 401(k)s, Roth IRAs, and taxable accounts).

Taxable accounts – Assets that are taxed immediately as opposed to retirement assets where tax is deferred.

Term life insurance – Life insurance that covers you for a fixed number of years. Often much less expensive than whole life insurance, term life insurance most commonly covers you for 10, 20, or 30 year terms, after which you would need to purchase a new policy if you still needed coverage.

Traditional IRA – As opposed to Roth IRAs, contributions to a Traditional IRA are in most cases tax deductible, and contributions and earnings are taxable when withdrawn in retirement. Withdrawals prior to age 59 ½ are subject to a 10% penalty. Traditional IRAs have strict eligibility requirements.

Variable annuity – A tax-deferred savings instrument in which the beneficiary makes an initial contribution today (or over a period of time) and receives an income stream for a period of time in the future (typically covering the beneficiary's lifetime). Unlike a fixed annuity, which provides a set amount each year, the amount provided by a variable annuity depends upon the investment return earned prior to the distribution period.

Vested – Refers to employer contributions to a retirement or stock option plan that have become legal property of the beneficiary. Most typically, a beneficiary becomes vested in a fixed portion of a plan's assets with each year of service.

Whole life insurance – A life insurance policy that typically remains in-force for the insured's entire life (as long as the annual premiums continue to be paid).

Acknowledgments

....

This book has been a labor of love and I have many people to thank for their part in the journey.

My staff at Stevens Wealth Management LLC and Financial Happiness LLC have helped through their support, comments and endless patience throughout this process. Thanks to Jason Guenther, Colleen Van Rossem, Nancy Wirth, Sara Connelly and Elaine Eakes. I thank Jason for his technical expertise, Colleen for her artistic eye on graphics, Nancy for her unfailing support, Elaine for all of her hard work on coordinating this book and Sara for twenty years of friendship and dedication.

Jim Eaton has done a fabulous job with graphics throughout this book. He brings artistry to these pages that elevate the whole project.

Janice Fried is responsible for the illustrations you see throughout the book and on the cover. I encourage you to see these in color at www.financial-happiness.com. They bring me great joy in their detail and imagination.

Kevin Laughlin is probably the best editor I know. I have been privileged to have his comments on this book. He is thoughtful, intelligent and a good friend.

Sam Horn has been my writing coach. We met at the Maui Writers Conference (now Hawaii Writers Conference) and we've worked on this project since 2008 in Fiji.

I am especially grateful for the privilege of working with such amazing clients over a twenty year period. I learn something every day and enjoy the creative work we are able to do together.

Anyone who has ever written a book or tackled a major project knows that it's not possible without support on the home front. I rely on Annette Letang, my personal assistant, to keep things running smoothly. She's unfailingly kind and a joy to my spirit. And thanks too to Jeremy Remmy who keeps me healthy—body, mind and spirit.

I also have to thank my loyal spiritual companions—a great group of people who I met through Caroline Myss's workshops who continue to meet monthly. I especially want to thank Heath Missner who has been a true spiritual director to me and has offered friendship and guidance.

I dedicated the book to my mom, Nancy Stevens. She has always encouraged me to follow my heart wherever it may lead. And I want to thank my brother Rick Stevens and his wife Rhoda Drije for their support and love over so many years. Although my dad, Richard Byron Stevens, passed away at age 50, he will always be part of my spirit as will the amazing women who greatly influenced my life: Margaret Leader, my grandmother, Charlotte Stevens, my grandmother, and Hazel Dame, my great-aunt.

I have had many wise teachers who unselfishly contributed to my success over the years—Dudley Powers, Howard Haas, Caroline Myss, Andrew Harvey are but a few. I am deeply appreciative for their love and support.

Made in the USA
Charleston, SC
18 December 2009